Whatever
Happened
to
John Henty?

To the Henty family worldwide

Save our Henty plea to Maggie

THE Prime Minister has been asked to join the mounting campaign to save Radio Sussex presenter John Henty from the chop.

His Early Bird show is due to be axed on May 1.

Fan Eric Muggeridge, 76, has written to Mrs Thatcher asking her to intervene.

The former travel agent, of Montpelier Place, Brighton, has also offered to start a collection to pay Henty's wages.

Mr Muggeridge said: "I'd even put a tenner a week of my own money to keep him on the air.

"I love the show and don't know what I shall do when it goes. It has been to me, as with many other people, the best tonic to start the day.

"I wrote to Mrs Thatcher because she is the sort of person who would take an interest in a matter like this. Something should be done."

Radio Sussex says Henty's show is going off the air for financial reasons, but it has not yet officially announced its decision.

Station manager John Saunders refused to comment on the growing anger about the decision to end the show.

But he did say: "The show will finish and the decision is final."

Henty, who has been connected with the station since it began 19 years ago as Radio Brighton, said today: "I'm very touched by Mr Muggeridge's concern.

"I've spoken to him a few times on the phone and regard him as a friend."

The programme is to be replaced by music and travel reports.   **27.4.87**

© John Henty, 2004

Cover design: Richard Marston
Cover photograph of John, Molly Gledhill and *Argus*: Hy Money

Published by Pomegranate Press
51 St Nicholas Lane, Lewes, Sussex BN7 2JZ
email: pomegranatepress@aol.com; website: pomegranate-press.co.uk

ISBN 0-9542587-7-0

British Library Cataloguing-in-Publication Data
A catalogue record for this book is available from the British Library

Printed by Antony Rowe Limited, Highfield Industrial Estate, Eastbourne, East Sussex BN23 6QT

FOREWORD

by Desmond Lynam

It's the beard – small, goatee-like, which has sat on the Henty chin for the 36 or so years that I have known him – that is the barometer of the man.

One stroke and he has found the germ of another idea, a programme, a cause, a journey.

Two strokes and it's already in fruition in one of the most agile minds I have ever met in the world of broadcasting.

John, with whom I began working in radio all those years ago, is very largely responsible for the career that I seem to have forged ever since, for which I can only apologise to him and to you.

Here is a man for whom fame was no spur; rather he wrote, broadcast, took up a cause simply because he believed in it wholeheartedly.

He is a wholly original talent who local radio gave voice to in the beginning – which set him on a fantastic journey to . . . well, I'll let John tell the story, but you'll be a better person for reading it.

"It's a terrible mistake to think that being famous is tantamount to being interesting"

– Andrew Solomon

Will silence prove golden for church?

by John Ryall

WHEN an Act of God such as the 1987 hurricane lumbers your church with a hellish repair bill, there are only two chaps it makes sense to turn to.

God, and John Henty.

The enterprising Mr Henty aims to raise urgently needed repair and restoration funds for 400-year-old Westgate Chapel at Lewes . . . by selling silence to the Americans.

The former BBC Radio Sussex producer and one-time presenter of the axed Early Bird breakfast show has recorded the peace and quiet inside the church on 60-minute audio cassettes.

Now Westgate's minister Jeremy Goring plans to swell church coffers by selling the tapes for £3.50 next time he visits the States.

Buyers can get down to 60 minutes of silence broken only by the noise of the wind and a piece of polythene flapping against a hurricane-damaged window.

But will Henty's silence prove golden? His last Transatlantic venture, selling the Americans tins of London fog, attracted considerable interest from American Customs, but little else.

"I had some difficulty with that one," he says. "In the end I gave the tins to someone as a present."

But he's confident that silence has the edge on fog. After all, it's not just any old silence. "It is a silence hallowed by the prayers of many generations."

Minister Jeremy Goring shares Henty's enthusiasm. "One of the main reasons people value Westgate is because it is a sanctuary of peace and quiet in an increasingly noisy world.

"We decided we could capture the tranquil atmosphere on tape and share it with others."

■ John Henty: tape bid to aid church

Variety is the spice of freelance life – and you don't always have to work for money. This is the Argus report of my wheeze of selling silence to the Americans to raise money for the 400-year-old Westgate Chapel in my present home town of Lewes.

PREFACE

Who swam the English Channel at the age of 12 in 1948 – despite suffering from chronic asthma?

Who gate-crashed a Buckingham Palace garden party in 1987 and sang 'Delilah' for the Queen Mother in pouring rain?

Who appeared on the stage of the London Palladium in 1965 dressed as the front half of a dromedary in the pantomime 'Aladdin', starring Cliff Richard and the Shadows?

Who was the subject of a 'This is Your Life' programme in 1998 which had to be abandoned because of a technicians' dispute at Thames Television?

We've no idea, but it certainly was *not* the subject of this somewhat strange autobiography.

Among the other things he also did *not* do:

John never wrote an unauthorised biography of comedian Jim Davidson entitled 'Lucky? I Must Have Nine Wives', and he never slept with a member of ABBA when they won the Eurovision Song Contest in Brighton in 1974.

However, he *did* fly to Istanbul with James Bond, visit Motown Studios in Detroit and interview the voice of Bugs Bunny, Mel Blanc, in Hollywood, AND he did offer to cut Spike Milligan's grass when the comedian visited his old mum in Australia, SO . . .

This is the unexpurgated story of a rather unusual life told in a rather unusual way.

WARNING for those who are easily offended: there are a couple of references to Simon Bates.

Hippy days – as John meets the wild bunch in California, 1960.

INTRODUCTION

Autobiographical is it, Mr . . .?

Henty – John Henty

Mmmmmmmmmm – not very commercial, HENTY, I'm afraid. I get an awful lot of people offering me their life stories you know – on average about four or five a week.

What ALL called Henty?

Please! It would help if you were well known or perhaps a minor celebrity.

Well, I did present programmes on the radio.

Oh they all say that. Hospital radio was it?

No it wasn't. BBC radio actually – both local and national. I worked with Simon Bates for a time . . .

I should keep quiet about that if I were you. About this name, then . . .

I think I ought to tell you that G.A. Henty – a writer of boys' adventure stories at the turn of the twentieth century – was the J.K. Rowling of his time. He sold millions of books all over the world and they're very collectable today.

Well, I'm sure they are John. Are you related to him, then?

Er, no, I'm not actually . . . Well I don't *think* so anyway

Perhaps you're related to J.K. Rowling. THAT would be useful.

'fraid not. I haven't even read a Harry Potter book.

Pity that – might help you in writing your book. Any magic in it?

I used to do conjuring and won a prize in Eastbourne for performing a disappearing coin trick at the Redoubt bandstand.

Not quite what I had in mind John. Do you know any witches perhaps?

Yes – in fact I regularly interviewed a white witch who was very knowledgeable on the subject of the occult and lived quietly in Brighton.

Did you visit her coven?

No – she had a council flat, and running around naked during the summer solstice was frowned upon in St. James's Street for some reason. Our house in another part of the city did have a ghost which made its presence known on a few occasions. I could elaborate on that if you like . . .

Good idea! That's what they want these days – plus lashings of sex, violence and celebrity. You know – 'Brighton on a Friday night' sort of thing. What did you say the working title of your book was?

Whatever Happened to John Henty? **It was the heading for a major feature which appeared in our local newspaper not so long ago. It just got me thinking about the wildly varied life that I've enjoyed over a 40-year career as a broadcaster and journalist. The people I've met, places I've visited, photographs I've taken . . . that sort of thing.**

Fair enough – although I have to say my immediate reaction to the question *What Happened to John Henty?* is a cynical 'Who cares?' Go on – prove me wrong, John. Let's have a few random examples and then perhaps a sample chapter. What sort of people did you meet, then?

The Beatles, Alfred Hitchcock, Charlton Heston, Mel Blanc who was the voice of Bugs Bunny, Stevie Wonder, Simon Bates . . .

I told you to drop him, John. What else ?

I flew to Istanbul with the James Bond Film Unit for 'From Russia With Love'; appeared on 'Double Your Money' with a chimpanzee and Hughie Green (in that order); emigrated to America; got stood up by Jackie Collins; had my tie cut in half by Roy Castle; and ran a shop and museum in Cornwall for four years. I paid Desmond Lynam a couple of quid for football reports and became a world authority on the life and times of childrens' illustrator, Mabel Lucie Attwell. I saw comedienne Nellie Wallace break her leg in a Bournemouth wartime pantomime and I've also been chairman of the Max Miller Appreciation Society. I've kept a day-to-day diary since the age of 11, and I've been married to the same woman for 40 years. Any more ?

No, that's fine, but apart from selling the idea to me you've got to be able to get your message across to the book-reading public as well. Do you think you can sell the weird world of John Henty to them? Public appearances, radio interviews, Parkinson – that sort of thing?

Not a problem! You're talking to a man who actually recorded and sold the Sound of Silence around the world – and I don't mean Simon and Garfunkle's version. It was a 30-minute audio cassette containing almost no sound at all apart from the wind whistling through the damaged window of a Unitarian chapel in East Sussex. The tape was used to raise money for restoration work to the chapel and was featured on all national radio networks in this country and abroad. Do you want to know more?

No, save it for the book, John. Sounds like another good story to me. OK, how about that all-important first chapter, then? And I think you'd better explain to casual readers how the cryptic title came about – then how *you* came about I guess . . .

1

My immediate reaction was – I don't believe this! I simply did not believe that I had chosen to live with my wife and son in a town where my great grandfather had been born 130 years before. Not only that, but we'd moved into the new terraced house in Kew Street, Brighton, only recently and the evidence before me in Somerset House on that fateful day suggested that Thomas Henty (for that was his name on the birth certificate) born February 1, 1845, had lived a stone's throw away at no. 17 Frederick Street for the first few years of his life.

Yet I had been totally unaware of the Henty family connection with Brighton when I applied for a job as a producer with one of the first local radio stations in this country – BBC Radio Brighton – in 1967. And we didn't even move to Brighton in the first place, because Sylvia and I, with our new baby son Andrew, were under some pressure to find a home quickly within the new station's editorial area before it opened in February 1968.

A small terraced property in nearby Shoreham-by-Sea was our first acquisition, but as the station developed and my role as sports and general producer proved more and more demanding, a move to be nearer the Marlborough Place studios became a priority. A new development in the very heart of the town – a mere five minutes walk away from the Royal Pavilion – came to our attention and we just about found enough funds to put down a deposit on no. 1 Kew Street – end of terrace, garage and all for just over £9,000. Believe me, that was a lot of money in the early seventies, and some of my radio colleagues were convinced I'd been left a sizeable sum by a rich relative or a relatively rich listener.

As you will discover in this investigation into *Whatever Happened To John Henty?* (I heard that madam – totally uncalled for!) my branch of the Sussex-based family was originally from east of the county and poor with it, while the West Sussex lot were considered landed gentry. In 1829, for example, while Thomas's dad, Samuel, aged 12, struggled with elementary schooling in the Seaford area, James Henty, the eldest son of farmer Thomas Henty from West Tarring, was manager of the family bank at Worthing and merchant in his own name as well. Charles, the second son, was manager of the family bank at Arundel and William was studying law at Lewes. The rest of the family lived down on the 3000-acre farm. That is, until they all decided to emigrate to Australia – to the Swan River Settlement, New South Wales, where they landed on October 12, 1829, having left England in June of that year. And – yes – their remarkable adventures in establishing themselves in the New World would not only make a good book but it has already been written and published in Australia under the title *The Hentys* by Lady Marnie Bassett (Oxford University Press 1954).

We will return to the more humble Hentys of East Sussex later in this book, but first perhaps, I should explain, as best I can, the reason for its teasing – some might say tempting – title. Tempting, that is, to exclaim loudly 'Who .....ing cares whatever happened to John Henty?!' Why, on more than one occasion I've even asked the same question myself! It's not for nothing that I was once described as a self-effacing pessimist by an exasperated female friend. Another – in Vienna – accused me of behaving 'so straight', and one journalist summed me up as being 'idiosyncratic of Brighton'. I had to look that one up and subsequently used it to sign letters to the *Daily Telegraph* about the prevalence of dog excrement in Rottingdean.

No – when the local daily paper in Brighton, the *Evening Argus* as it was then in September 2000, decided to carry a weekend feature on John Henty, I imagined it was because they were running low of local celebs in the 'silly season' for newspapers. (There you go again John, running yourself down). Additionally, they may have been puzzled by the fact that after 20 years of regular broadcasting on parish pump radio my 'Early Bird Show' between 5.30 and 6.30 in the morning had been unceremoniously axed by the BBC. Then silence, prompting one listener (probably *the* listener – ooops, sorry!) to approach me in a local supermarket soon afterwards with the inevitable question: 'You used to be John Henty, didn't you?'

This, I suspect, is what feature writer Vanora Leigh was alluding to when she interviewed me at length in my home in Lewes on a warm summer's day a couple of years later. As far as broadcasting was concerned, I pointed out that freelance presenters (I left BBC staff in 1978) were always going to be vulnerable, and it seemed that the more popular the programme, the more exposed the person responsible for it.

I was paid £70 a week to get up at 4.30 in the morning for the one-hour show, I told Vanora, and yet the BBC management claimed that the programme was discontinued for 'financial reasons'. Not very convincing – especially as they were forced to replace the programme with speech and music anyway, such was the outcry from Early Bird listeners to its dubious demise. One charming fellow even got round to petitioning the prime minister, Margaret Thatcher. Local politicians were also involved, plus Age Concern representatives who were concerned on behalf of their older clients who regarded the programme as 'a friend'.

But I digress – and be warned, dear reader, that I'm rather good at it. Yes, the *Argus* article may have satisfied the odd supermarket shopper confronted by a bearded ex-broadcaster who looked vaguely familiar. For me, though – at a point in my life where a lively past had much more appeal than the prospect of a fragile future – a decision was made. I'd write a book about this John Henty character – the senior aircraftsman, the local newspaper reporter, the third pirate on the left, the emigrant, the husband, the father, the broadcaster, the leading art authority and the generally all-round 'nice' – if rather straight – guy.

Do that John, I said to myself, and even YOU might begin to believe some of the stories. Go on – give it a try . . .

2

So – how did it all start? 'At number 138 Brigstock Road in Thornton Heath, South London' is, I'm afraid, the rather disappointing answer, but don't worry, it does get better, and NO there *isn't* a plaque on the wall today to mark the event – despite numerous letters I've written to the council over the years.

John Frederick Henty, the only child of Lionel and Florence Henty of South Croydon, was born in a private nursing home on Wednesday, 25th of March in 1936 – the same year, you may be interested to know, that the Crystal Palace burned down in Upper Norwood a few miles away from Brigstock Road. Norbury Police confirmed later that there was no link between the two events.

The happy parents (well I hope they were) had married in Fulham, West London, 18 months previously. 'Peggy', as my mother was known, was a telephone operator at the Whitehall Exchange close by Trafalgar Square in London. Lionel was described on my birth certificate as a commercial clerk with a petroleum company.

Dad was employed by the Shell Petroleum Company for most of his working life and spent ten years abroad in Borneo involved with oil exploration for the Dutch-owned company. He frequently gave me the impression that he enjoyed those bachelor years thousands of miles from his family home in Croydon. He was the only son of Fred and Kate Henty who also had three daughters, Eva, Muriel and Eunice.

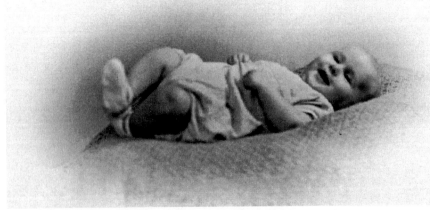

The infant John Henty, South Croydon 1936.

In Borneo my father worked hard and played hard. He was a popular man in the all-important social circle of white European oil workers. His nickname was 'Twink', and he was no mean sportsman either. In fact, before setting-off for the Far East he even played, as an amateur, on one occasion for Crystal Palace Football Club. I still have the tatty, four-paged programme to verify the fact and our family association with the quixotic south London club continues even today.

It was playing cricket, however, that changed my father's life irreparably, and one of his former colleagues in Borneo told me it altered his outgoing personality too. The full details of his accident aren't known – my father was never wildly forthcoming to me about any close personal matters – but it seems that he was batting on a matting pitch when the bat he was using split and somehow a part of it shot upwards and entered his left eye.

In south suburban London this would have been serious enough. In the wilds of Sarawak, Borneo, it was a disaster. Dad was whisked away aboard an oil tanker (he told my wife he was winched up the side of the ship, strapped to a stretcher) and several days later arrived in Singapore. He lost the eye and was immediately fitted with a very realistic glass one. In fact so realistic that I was 10 or 11 years of age before I realised that it was not real, a school friend pointing this out to me.

The loss of this one eye obviously meant that my father needed to return to the United Kingdom and soon, in the early 1930s, he was working for Shell in the City of London as an accountant. I imagine that the weary routine of a 9-to-5 job in Bishopsgate (with a daily commute by train from East Croydon to London Bridge) must have seemed like a very poor substitute for the freedom and adventure of oil exploration among the Dayaks of North Borneo.

It also meant that initially he was living back home in Bramley Close, South Croydon, with Ma and the girls. The head of the family, Fred Henty, was a commercial traveller for the North British Rubber Company and, significantly I feel, he spent much of his time on the road – away from the matriarchal home. My father in his turn sought his escape by getting married, and he and my mother started life together in a brand new – typical 30s – mock-Tudor house with garage and garden in Whitgift Avenue, South Croydon. I believe it cost somewhere in the region of £400, which was a considerable sum of money in those modest days. I have no idea what my father earned in the mid-30s, but I do recall that when I started work for Shell some 16 years later his lifetime target for me was to reach ultimately £1000 a year.

How things have changed. The world was changing too for Peggy Alderman, my mother, who was born Florence Agnes in Lots Road, Chelsea, in April 1907. Her father, Henry Francis, was described as a 'paper hanger' on her birth certificate and Peggy had a younger sister, Norah. Their mother Agnes died at the age of 34 in 1920 and Mr. Alderman subsequently re-married, to a woman I knew only as 'Mrs Harris'.

For 29-year old Mrs. Henty, life in a detached house in Croydon with a new baby son must have contrasted greatly with her working life in a busy London telephone exchange. Mum would tell me of the fun the operators had, for example, saying 'Rubber knees' to callers instead of the standard 'Number, please'. Now she found herself on the other end of the line (CROydon 7544) alone with a demanding child and a husband off to the city more than likely six days a week. Add to that the probably unwanted attention of a mother-in-law just around the corner and one can imagine perhaps that early days of married life were not entirely a bed of roses.

Obviously I can remember very little of this life in Whitgift Avenue before the onset of the Second World War in September 1939. Eight years on – in 1947 – I started keeping the first of many day-to-day diaries, but at the tender age of three my only point of reference today is an album of family photographs taken at the time. Many of these – in sepia and black and white –were taken in the long, rear garden of number 21 which backed onto the grounds of Whitgift School in Haling Park. My father, who had attended Whitgift Middle School

Cheerful, chubby little chap with 'Ted' the penguin and my dad.

in the centre of Croydon, was obviously intent on his son receiving a public school (albeit independent public school) education.

But that was for the future. As a cheerful, chubby little chap pedalling furiously across the lawn on his Triang tricycle and sharing a model car with favoured 'Ted' and passenger Penguin, the present was all about summer days in South Croydon, with the occasional holiday in Herne Bay on the Kentish coast.

If you asked me for my earliest personal memory of those seemingly halcyon days before the war, I can just about recall an incident in the Classic cinema, South Croydon, when a screaming – and I mean screaming – John Henty had to be hurriedly removed from the Circle of the tiny cinema. It was my first ever visit to the 'pictures', and I think a moment when American ventriloquist Edgar Bergen had a jug of water unceremoniously poured over his head by Charlie (his doll) proved too realistic by far for this Little John.

It was several years later before anyone could persuade me to enter the 'dark, sinister' confines of a picture house, and even then the broomstick sequence in Disney's 'Fantasia' had me scurrying for the exit. Such a sensitive child – or was I?

I was certainly an only child, but I can honestly say that I never regarded this as an impediment to a happy childhood. Neither was I ever LONELY, and in many ways I rather enjoyed my own company – inventing characters to play with and, in Southbourne, devising my own radio programmes which I often 'broadcast' (from my bed to my parents on the same floor: it was a bungalow) before going to sleep. Apparently, they could only stop the show by 'turning me off' and shouting 'CLICK!' – a foretaste of things to come perhaps?

I was also very keen on our sizeable radiogram with one 78 record getting repeated plays: 'Little Man You've Had A Busy Day'. It must have summed up my South Croydon life perfectly. Unbeknown to me, however, this was all to change, explaining my earlier reference to the seaside town of Southbourne, to the east of Bournemouth in Hampshire. Within months we were to move there. The outbreak of the Second World War was imminent.

3

While I enjoyed listening to the radio, even at the age of three, I cannot recall hearing the fateful broadcast by Prime Minister, Neville Chamberlain, when he announced to the nation – on the morning of September 3rd 1939 – that we were at war with Germany. Oddly enough, the sound of the air-raid warning siren that followed soon after in Croydon (and our waiting for hours for something to happen before agreeing that it was a false alarm) remains with me to this day.

Otherwise the notion of 'war' simply meant upheaval to this child and I had no comprehension of some evil nation intent on invading my homeland or killing me and my parents in our beds. Of more concern to jolly John Henty was the fact that bananas were no longer on the breakfast menu – preferably mashed with milk and sugar. Oh, and it would become increasingly difficult for mum and dad to buy me my favourite Christmas annuals – 'Chick's Own' and 'Tiny Tots' – because of the 'shortage of paper for non-essential purposes'.

For my father – nearing the age of 40 and only having the use of one eye – a 'call up' for military service was out of the question and he, and others like him in Shell, found themselves moving out of London, with their families, to the relative peace and quiet of Branksome Chine, west of Bournemouth, where they provided support from the oil industry to the country's hard-pressed armed services.

Like so many things in his life, this was work which he never discussed with me, so – again – I was blissfully innocent of the pressures and perils of war. Perhaps this is what he intended, for certainly the first two years of the conflict were the most hazardous for us on the 'home front' with the nightly bombing of London and other major cities, the Battle of Britain and the very real threat of invasion from across the channel.

The only evidence I saw of this were the ugly anti-tank barriers which were quickly erected along the beautiful sandy coastline stretching from Southbourne to Bournemouth and beyond. Even the noisy blowing up of both Bournemouth and Boscombe piers at night never fully alerted me to the imminent dangers of 20th century warfare. The move to the seaside had to be 'good news' for this south suburban child, and soon the small Henty family was living in a rented, detached bungalow in Paisley Road, Southbourne. Whitgift Avenue remained empty.

The banana that was not a bomb

Again, the small number of photographs (film was almost impossible to find in wartime) show a cheerful child picking apples in a cramped back garden and enjoying an outdoor birthday party with new-found friends from Southbourne High School. I suppose Anne and Mary were my very first 'girlfriends', and I do recall fairly innocent games of exploration involving 'doctors and nurses' in the family garage.

Typically perhaps, it was the promise of beetroot sandwiches prepared by their mum for our tea after a game in Fisherman's Walk that impressed me more than the curious attentions of her two daughters. My love of bananas too was fairly common knowledge in the war, and imagine my surprise when Mary approached me in Castlemaine Avenue one afternoon and coyly offered one such piece of delicious fruit.

'Mr Palmer, the butcher in Kimberley Road, has come home on leave from the Far East,' she told me, 'and he raffled this banana. I won it but you can have it John 'cos I know you like bananas – don't you?'

Well, yes I did, but I'd also heard that that dreadful man Hitler was currently dropping familiar-looking objects into British streets from the sky, only for them to explode when picked up by innocent boys and girls. Could this exotic looking object be such an evil device?

With Mary's assurance that Mr. Palmer was not a German spy and that her banana had not fallen out of the sky, I sped off home to mum in the bungalow and we debated long and hard whether I should eat it in one piece, cut it into slices or mashed with sugar and 'top of the milk'.

You can guess which one I chose – and it was definitely NOT a bomb.

4

My wartime schooling as such was very much hit and miss, and I don't mean my being hit by the indomitable Miss Fort. In fact she was an excellent teacher at Southbourne High School and certainly taught me the basic 3 R's with kindness, consideration and concern. Arithmetic was just not my scene, I soon discovered, and, in the exercise book which I still have, there are far more blue crosses than red ticks indicating a correct answer to a sum. Writing, though, was another matter entirely and once I'd got the hang of stringing all the carefully-formed letters together, stories flowed from the Henty pencil, and later – at the tender age of eight – I'd even written a thriller entitled 'Murder Is The Word!' which was submitted to Uncle Jack, editor of my favourite 'Tiny Tots' comic.

He must have been puzzled by this unlikely offering and wrote in reply: 'I think it is very good for eight years old. As you say your story is a bit blood-thirsty – a little too exciting for 'Tiny Tots'. If you go on as you have started, I think there is every chance that you may one day write a

My Tiny Tots Order of Merit, which allows me to use the letters TTOM after my name – even today!

novel and get it published.' He concluded: 'Well, goodbye little friend. In ten years time I shall be looking for 'Murder Is The Word' on the bookstalls. It is a good title and one that suits the taste of reading today. Good Luck! Uncle Jack.'

I still have this hand-written letter and the Tiny Tots Order of Merit on a postcard which accompanied it. Uncle Jack pointed out that members of the order may use the letters T.T.O.M. after their names, and I have been known to do just that some 50 years on when seeking to impress officialdom! Amazingly it works, and provides ample compensation for regularly being left out of HM's birthday honours list. Who needs an MBE when you've got a far more unique TTOM?

Life in Southbourne during the early years of the war was innocent enough. I learned to ride a bicycle in Fisherman's Walk – close by the bandstand in the centre. I travelled on a yellow trolley bus into Bournemouth with mum to visit the big department store Beales before it was bombed. I enjoyed my first pantomime at the Pavilion Theatre when comedienne Nellie Wallace sang 'I Don't Want To Set The World On Fire' and promptly fell over, breaking her leg. I played with John Burt, Terry and Penny in Herberton Road, and it was through their persistence that I was persuaded to re-enter a cinema to see 'Fantasia' for someone's birthday treat. Not mine.

Because of the uncertainties of war, my mother and I returned to Croydon at one point to 'escape' the possible invasion threat to the south coast, only to find that we were under even greater danger in Croydon, which had become the focal point for un-manned V1 and V2 rockets. With their totally indiscriminate nature, these 'flying bombs', as they were known, became a terrifying prospect for the people of south London – night after night. At the sound of the air raid warning, we made for the pantry, which extended under the stairs in Whitgift Avenue, and stayed there in cramped conditions on a mattress until the 'All Clear' sounded. Later, we acquired an enormous Anderson shelter which was a steel structure somehow erected in the front lounge. When my father shared it with us he was for ever banging his balding head on the very solid roof section. I found this amusing. He didn't.

In Croydon, for a short spell, I attended Coombe Hill House in Park Lane – a preparatory school for boys – run by a rather stern husband and wife team, the Uphills. Just as I was settling in and again making new friends, it was decided (by whom I do not know) that we should return to Southbourne and there, bizarrely, I became a pupil of Portsmouth

Grammar School, which had had to remove from Portsmouth itself because of the heavy bombing there.

For reasons that are quite beyond recall now, this brief Portsmouth phase in my increasingly erratic education brought out the best in me. A book prize for 'keen endeavour' was one reward and – even better – I was chosen to read out passages from a popular book to the whole class during the frequent absence of one woman teacher. This I thoroughly enjoyed, and as it happened on more than one occasion it seems that my class mates also appreciated the effort. At least they didn't riot.

Even at my early age, mum (with her telephone operator experience) had always impressed on me to 'speak nicely' and this I attempted to do – combining it with a sense of humour, the odd dramatic flourish and the occasional bit of showing-off. Oh, I loved an audience and the buzz that I received from this brief episode clearly remained with me into early adult life. After all, just add a microphone and you've got the makings of a potential broadcaster.

Radio, of course, was at its peak during the wartime and we would sit around the wireless in the evenings as a family, listening to Tommy Handley in 'ITMA', 'Monday Night At Eight', 'The Brains Trust' and, importantly, the frequent news bulletins. For me, 'Children's Hour' (between five and six o'clock) was sacrosanct, too. My impersonations of Larry The Lamb and Mr Grouser from 'Toy Town' are still valid today (if a trifle obscure), and I adored Norman and Henry Bones, the boy detectives, 'Mompty' and 'Peckham' and one series from the BBC in Wales which I think was called, ominously, 'The Valley Of Om'. Magical stuff, and how privileged we were to have had the benefit of such fine programmes in what must have been at times impossible circumstances.

My own circumstances were about to change yet again, but for all the right reasons. The war in Germany was over (hooray – bananas for breakfast!) and I can recall the excitement in May 1945 when 'Victory' over Japan was announced on the radio and a man leant out of his first floor window in Beaufort Road and shouted the joyous news to mum and me, who were passing at the time. Croydon (again), a brief return to Coombe Hill House and then the entrance examination to the school at the bottom of our garden – Whitgift.

I was to become an ever-so-unlikely public school boy.

5

Today Whitgift School in South Croydon is as good an example of an independent public school as you will find anywhere in the United Kingdom. Its academic results are outstanding, its sporting achievements are exceptional and, above all else, it caters for the individual in all aspects of creative living. I envy the 21st century Whitgiftians with their world tours, drama productions involving real girls and trendy school magazine.

In 1946 things were not like that at all and I have to say, in many ways, I found it an alien, unwelcoming world. The newly-arrived headmaster, E.A.G. Marlar, led a pretty disparate team of teaching staff, all male and many of them fresh from military service abroad. It showed. I won't name names, but I can remember one or two who appeared permanently shell-shocked (perhaps they were), while others were alarmingly aggressive at times. The older members of staff tolerated the newcomers but no more. Marlar favoured corporal punishment and it was freely administered on a regular basis. This is dubious enough when carried out by teachers, but it was totally wrong when performed – with great enthusiasm – by prefects (many of them no older than their 'victims') at weekly Prefects' Court.

As far as I know, never having been a prefect, Marlar laid down no guidelines for this belligerent behaviour and, clearly, what went on behind a closed, panelled door didn't concern him. It certainly concerned us though, as pupils, and I can remember the fear of standing outside the prefects' room on a Friday lunchtime awaiting my turn to face the 'Court'. On one occasion – and there weren't too many of them I hasten to add – I even smuggled a bible into the room, to swear upon it that I was 'not guilty' of exploding a brown paper bag at the end of one long House meeting: 'Not me, guv – must've been someone else!' It worked, and I ended up with writing out a hundred lines of some nonsense or other.

I still meet one or two of those prefects at school reunions now. One was a famous England test cricketer, another went on to be headmaster at an even more famous public school. They may have turned out to be pillars of society but at school they were bullies, shamefully sanctioned by the headmaster.

I survived in the junior school at least by being an eccentrically likeable child. Latin teacher Claud Loving in room 1 took a shine to me in the nicest possible way, always asking the same question on grammar.

'Henty – come out here and tell us about the verb to be.'

'Yes, sir' I would chirp, 'The verb to be is the commonest verb of incomplete predication (*pause, and then triumphantly*) and takes a nominative complement.'

'Quite right Henty. Have a sheet of blotting paper!'

Amo, Amas, Amat was fine, but anything beyond that was a complete mystery. General Science too was a no-go area, although I did enjoy the occasional search for plant- or insect-life in the sprawling school grounds. At least we were out of the classroom. The biology teacher was also the head of the junior school, and all I will say about him – in retrospect – is that he was very 'hands-on' and would not have survived in todays' wisely more cautious world. As it was, the man left Whitgift, shall we say, under a cloud and surrounded by rumours that I would not choose to substantiate 50 years on.

Homosexuality was not unknown, of course, but was treated in a fairly jocular way by most of my schoolboy contemporaries. It was not so much a matter of fancying another pupil, more a question of being curious about your own and others' sexuality. Masters in the main were considered 'straight' in a military sort of way. Girls, of course, were very much an unknown quantity – unless you had a sister – and matters were made much worse when it came to staging productions of Shakespeare or Gilbert and Sullivan operas.

For example, I made a very unconvincing schoolgirl from Titipu in The Mikado, and none of us in the 'female' chorus-line could understand why we needed to keep our knees together so much when sitting down. Girls were rarely seen in Haling Park then, and when they did arrive – for a sporting event – to sit tantalisingly atop a grass bank watching cricket perhaps, some of us positioned ourselves below in the hope of spying the odd stocking top . . . or more. It was certainly of greater interest than the cricket from what I remember, and the girls seemed to enjoy it too. Voyeurism is all very well, but at 15 it was a poor substitute for the real thing, and for John Henty that raunchy reality was a long, long way off.

For starters, apart from being naive, I was also what can only be described as fat, although my friends preferred to call me 'Chunky' – the nickname of one of the cheery school groundsmen. Unbeknown to me, BBC TV was planning a series of childrens' programmes based on the Billy Bunter stories penned by Frank Richards. One of my pals submitted my name to the producer, Joy Harrington, and I was amazed to get an invitation to attend Lime Grove Studios in West London, for an audition.

Until then, my only acting experience had been in a one-act play, written and performed in French, called 'L'Inspecteur Arrive', in which my character – the class 'grass' – had to point accusingly towards another child with the words 'C'est Pierre!' Apart from the fact that I was then set upon by the entire cast, I enjoyed the experience and had no fears of auditioning for the mighty BBC.

It all went very well. I squeaked and squealed my way through several pages of script, ate the odd bun or two (no problem) and got on with Ms Harrington like a house on fire. Of course, they gave the job ultimately to a professional actor – the not-so-cuddly Gerald Campion – but I received a signed copy of a Bunter book and the acclamation of my pals back in form RB1.

And if I have an axe to grind about the role Whitgift played in my future development, it is that I believe the potential was there but never

exploited or properly explored. Yes, I did become a journalist, broadcaster and travel writer, but none of these achievements was a direct result of encouragement from teaching staff at Haling Park. I edited a form magazine entitled *Whitgift Times*, appeared on a 'Twenty Questions' panel at a junior school Christmas party and organised the one meeting of the 'Conjuror's Club' in which Colin and I took people's subscriptions only to pay them back at the headmaster's hurried behest! I joined and left earlier than I should the C.C.F (Combined Cadet Force), never scored a try at rugby yet scored numerous goals with a tennis ball in the playground – where I was known as the 'Flying Plum Pudding'.

'Stand at ease!' I left Whitgift's CCF earlier than I should.

Academically I struggled, and I still feel that over 30 boys in each class meant that any form of personal tuition was almost out of the question. When I did receive one-to-one help to re-take my 'O' level mathematics examination, I passed with flying colours and this was due entirely to the patience of a Mr Stothard, who deserves a special mention in these despatches. He liked me and I liked him. It helped. And Messrs. Parsons, Tolman and Smith are also worthy of credit, but otherwise . . .

So I never made the safer, saner shores of the sixth form. Five 'O' levels were clearly the limit of my scholastic achievements. My father reckoned it was time for me to get a job, and there was a sad inevitability about my first employer – although I'm sure Lionel Frederick Thomas didn't see it that way. Shell had treated him well enough with service abroad and stability at home. If it was good enough for him then it would be good enough for me. After all, National Service was on the horizon and a job for life was everyone's goal, wasn't it? You can be sure of Shell!

Well no dad, actually. It certainly wasn't my goal, but what I find rather alarming now is the fact that I cannot remember having any say in the matter of my career choice. At witless Whitgift – on a wet Saturday morning – I was asked by the deputy headmaster what I was intending to do on leaving the school. I vividly recall answering: 'Broadcast, sir. I'm going to be a broadcaster.'

And what did he say to this outright statement? He didn't – moving on swiftly to another puzzled pupil. And that was it.

'Oh, there goes the bell. Dismiss!'

6

Hounsditch Warehouse on a January Monday morning in 1953 and my first day in full-time employment with the Shell Petroleum Company Limited. My father was actually working on another floor in the same soul-less building but I don't remember us travelling there together from Croydon. On arrival at Shell Court, its official title, I was soon designated to the export department (which later became purchasing department) on the second floor.

Open-plan offices were an unusual innovation in this country during the early 1950s and my first impression of the enormous floor space full of desks, ducts and anonymous people was not encouraging. In fact, it frightened the living daylights out of me from day one. And, worse still, there were what I can only describe as the Amazons of Administration. People of the Opposite Sex – and remember, I hadn't encountered too many of them at Whitgift – who were in charge of one or two of the sections responsible for records and filing. I was simply not used to being told what to do and where to go by a woman and, on that first, frantic day it came as a great cultural shock to me.

One of the younger 'worker bees', Iris, took pity on this bewildered, bespectacled 16-year-old and for the first few weeks – let alone days – shared the onerous duties of sorting out all the invoices, requisitions and purchase orders. It was extremely dull stuff involving pipelines at Pernis, cat-crackers (don't ask) and flanges, gaskets and the occasional kitchen sink. I hated it – loathed every minute of it – and became increasingly self-conscious, to a point where I simply would not enter the basement staff canteen. You've heard of factory farming ? Well, I was the victim of factory filing!

I felt that my every move was being monitored. Even to go to the relative privacy of the vast washrooms on each floor meant walking down long corridors between the various sections, clutching your regulation towel, observed every inch of the way. Or at least, that's how I saw it. Remarkably, I still have nightmares about those horrendous days and it took me ages to get over the excruciating self-consciousness of it all.

People who know me now are amazed to learn that even entering a crowded room or taking an underground journey then caused me great anxiety. This lasted all of 18 months, and although I viewed two years of

National Service with equal apprehension, at least it meant an escape from the 9-to-5 dread of purchasing department purgatory. Oh I made friends there eventually. Iris was a pal throughout, and I even got to work with the shapely Miriam and her friend, Gloria without blushing quite so frequently. Some of the 'buyers', I think they were called, befriended me, and the younger ones talked football and told me of their own dreams and aspirations. Many indicated a strong desire to get away from the all-powerful grip of the 'scallop' (or corporate Shell) themselves, and I listened avidly.

My chance to escape would come, I assured myself, and serving Queen and country could provide the time I needed to think up an alternative career plan. It was pretty obvious to me that if I didn't devise a scheme, I was facing 40 years of unadulterated Shell – without the 'S'. Sorry, dad. Roll on the call-up papers and goodbye Hounsditch – not au revoir.

The buff-coloured envelope duly arrived on Thursday, June 24th, 1954, following a medical and intelligence test at some remote hall in West Croydon. There, after a brief interview, I was accepted for the Royal Air Force with grade 1 for health.

It was generally accepted that this form of two-year National Service would soon be ended, but that was not going to help me in July 1954. Fourteen years earlier, young men like me had joined the RAF to become known as 'The First Of The Few'. The only valid epithet for my enforced enlistment was that I probably qualified as 'The Last Of The Many'.

7

Two weeks from receiving the call-up papers, I was on a train steaming out of London, bound for RAF Cardington in Bedfordshire, fully aware of the fact that my life was about to change in a very big way and that there was absolutely nothing I could do about it. Helpless ? Yes, it would seem so, yet I soon discovered that when faced with adversity, total strangers respond – almost instinctively – by helping one another. Those first few days were chaotic, of course. More medicals ('Cough!'), hideous haircuts, ill-fitting uniforms (hilarious berets) and much worse was yet to come. In my case, the hell of Hounsditch was about to be replaced by the horrors of Hednesford – a basic training camp on Cannock Chase, just outside the Midland town of Walsall.

We were transferred there by coach. It was raining hard, and the moment we clambered off the vehicle, harsh, strident voices started shouting at us. They never stopped for eight weeks – and neither did the rain. However, for AC2 Henty there was a fortuitous respite from the ranting and raving when a reddish rash arrived one Saturday morning in August (on my chest, dear reader, on my chest) which proved to be a very virulent form of chicken pox. Innocently, I presented myself on sick parade in a room full of ailing recruits, only to be rushed away by ambulance to an isolation hospital the moment my 'heat rash' was correctly diagnosed.

'Get that airman OUT of here!' the duty medic shouted (they all shouted it seemed), and off I went, bemused but not unduly worried – at least I was missing some dreaded ground combat training with the RAF Regiment that morning.

Compared to billet life on Cannock Chase, the isolation unit at nearby RAF Cosford was nigh on Nirvana. Not that I remember much about the first 48-hours or so, drugged to the eyeballs as I was and snug, too, in a proper bed with clean white sheets. Once the itching had subsided and contact made with home ('Don't worry mum, it's only chicken pox'; 'Chicken, dear? This is a bad line!') I began to take in my immediate surroundings and noticed, with my fellow patients, a similar billet to our own, set at a safe distance from us, which seemed to house – wait for it – *women*, some of whom waved at us as we stared across the divide. Whether this is true or not, I shall never know, but when we enquired about our near-neighbours, a male orderly tut-tutted and mumbled words to the effect that the building was a VD clinic and the women were all suffering from sexually-transmitted diseases. This may, of course, have been a far from subtle ploy on the part of our (was he gay?) medical friend to ensure that we kept our distance, but all I can say now is that it worked. Not that I was particularly interested in waylaying 'promiscuous' members of the WRAF . . . or the orderly! In fact, with my limited knowledge of sexual matters and the female psyche (things improve soon), John Henty was probably more at risk from them than they were from his spotty presence next door.

A couple of weeks passed blissfully at Cosford until it was felt I was fit enough to return to basic-training at Hednesford, and before that, according to our orderly friend, I was due seven-days sick leave at home. At this point in my short airforce career, a suitable subtitle for the book I was planning on National Service would have been 'Two Years Before the MO'.

After Cosford, though, my health and general well-being improved enormously and – like thousands of others who went through a similar 'military' experience – I actually began to enjoy the camaraderie of camp life. (Not that sort: I still fancied girls, even if I didn't know what to with 'em.). As a result of the 'illness' I was 'back-flighted' on my return to Hednesford and eventually passed out with a new bunch of recruits under the guidance of a more genial NCO. He liked us and, miraculously, we tolerated him. This was not always the case.

One corporal in the RAF regiment, exasperated by my handling of a bren gun, shouted me out in front of at least two flights of recruits.

'If you put your fingers there, airman, they'll be chopped off – and that's not the only thing if I join in!' he bellowed, 'You, airman, are as thick as shit in the neck of a bottle! What are you?'

Amidst howls of laughter, I repeated his insult, and that would have been the end of it except that the remark was also repeated by another 'sprog' airman when he was at home on leave in London. Unfortunately he told a senior member of his local air cadet force, and this prompted a letter to the Air Ministry suggesting that recruits were being subjected to foul and abusive language during basic training. An inquiry was called for, and at Hednesford I was ordered to identify the angry NCO – they even organised an identity parade of regiment instructors. They were a pretty tough bunch, believe me, and there was no way I was going to point the finger at any one of them. After all, it could be argued that I was lucky to have any fingers to point with anyway. To satisfy the embarrassing inquiry – and presumably Air Ministry minions – I signed a statement which effectively said that, while the remark had indeed been made, it was justified under the circumstances and was said in a humorous way. That was my story and I stuck to it. Phew!

I eventually escaped Hednesford aboard a bus full of hefty rugby players bound for an inter-camp match at RAF Hereford. This was where I had been posted following basic training, and the idea was to teach me – and hundreds of others like me – typing and the basics of office administration. To do this we sat at a bank of ancient typewriters and bashed away on the battered keyboards for hours on end. To the weird accompaniment of rhythmic music from a gramophone, we tackled touch-typing, laid out lengthy letters and learned the intricacies of the Official Secrets Act.

There are those who argue that for most conscripts, National Service was a complete waste of time. Others today contend, however, that it could be the answer to the indiscipline and indolence of so many contemporary young people – girls as well as boys. From my two years' experience in uniform, I would subscribe to the latter view. Typing was not the only thing I learned in the Royal Air Force. I accepted a discipline into my life. I enjoyed the company of a wide variety of people of my age from all over the United Kingdom. I acquired independence and appreciated the pleasures of home whenever I returned there on leave. And yes, I also cursed this enforced incarceration at times and counted the number of days left before 'demob' – just like everybody else.

When I left Hereford on Thursday, 24th February, 1955, there was still a very long way to go. 500 days' worth to be precise.

8

I can think of worse places to spend a good part of those 500 days though. Headquarters (Unit) No. 23 Group, Flying Training Command (how many times did I type those words? I wonder) was based around a large house – Oxendon House – approximately two miles from the centre of a market town, Leighton Buzzard, in Bedfordshire. Married quarters and the airman's mess, where we had all our meals, were located a short distance up Plantation Road. Our billets were scattered about in the grounds of the country house and we would be woken most mornings by the sounds of activity on the nearby canal. In many ways it was an idyllic setting – especially in the summer months.

I arrived late on a Sunday afternoon in early March 1955 and found the place almost deserted apart from an RAF policeman on the gate who directed me to my new home among the rhododendrons. There I met the weekend duty chef, who immediately offered to cook me something 'after my long journey'. Only from Croydon actually, but it was teatime and I was hungry. He arrived in the billet ten minutes later with a plate full of tomatoes on toast, albeit tinned tomatoes and soggy toast, but the gesture was a welcoming one and prompted this poem several years later.

> *Tinned tomatoes for tea*
> *Toast from under the grill*
> *Tinned tomatoes for tea*
> *The corporals's name is Bill.*
>
> *'Bin in for long?'*
> *He asks, with a grin.*
> *'I've only got these . . .'*
> *And points to a tin.*
>
> *Tinned tomatoes for tea.*
>
> *'It's not a bad place –*
> *Bit out of the way . . ..*
> *Didn't catch your name.*
> *Er, mine's Bill by the way.'*

I resist the lures of Billy Graham

'Group captain's a right one
But then they all are!
How baht a gherkin?
I've just opened the jar.'

'Course, it's quiet at the moment,
The weekend and that.
Soon be back from their passes.
'ere, I've no time to chat.'

'Still
Scrub up when you're finished
And bring back the plate . . ..
Those tommies are tempting,
But I'll just have to wait.'

My job in Sergeant Browning's orderly room was to create what were known as SROs – station routine orders. It was a bit like producing a weekly newsletter and I quite enjoyed the responsibility and challenge. Everybody had to read SROs because they contained details of parades, postings and pay. The orderly room was 'where it all happened', and there was a buzz about the place which I found invigorating.

The months passed innocently enough. I organised a coach trip to see the American big band led by Stan Kenton at a ballroom in Luton. A colleague, Terry, attempted to convert everybody – bussing us to a Billy Graham rally in London – and for two weeks I was shipped off to Munchen Gladbach in Germany where we lived in tents as part of a NATO exercise to assess our readiness for a nuclear attack. This was fine. We enjoyed the German beer, but people were not amused when told that the mobile NAAFI in the woods had closed after being hit by a nuclear device. We felt that this was an unlikely eventuality. Two weeks of fire fighting in Lancashire, gas attacks in Gloucestershire and a psychology course in Nottingham: the two years passed, and it was a very different John Henty who returned to the Shell Petroleum Company at the beginning of July 1956. I'd lived a bit.

I attended an interview in the public relations department at No. 1 Kingsway (having made it quite clear that there was no way I would ever return to Hounsditch Warehouse). 'I want a job where I meet the public,' I told the ever-so-slightly perplexed personnel bod in the city. He pointed me in the direction of public relations, which also incorporated the prestigious Shell photographic and film units. I noted in my diary: 'Pleasant surroundings – 8 floors up – job rather non-descript but could act as a useful stepping stone for the future.' And so it proved. It also introduced me to the delights of a new phenomenon: the typing pool.

With my newly-acquired typing experience and urgent desire for other more sensuous experiences, here was the seventh floor answer to my bachelor prayers – girls on tap! ('On tap mother, not top! This really is a bad line.') But would I *be* their type, and how was I to learn which keys to press and in what order so to speak. Very good questions and I needed to find out the answers pretty damn quick if my early attempts at 'courting' were anything to go by. A peck on the cheek from Judy and holding hands with Susan were not what I had in mind.

Meantime, I had decided to become 'something in PR'.

9

It was close-by the drinking water fountains in the Junior Playground that gangling Colin (the boy who helped me form the ill-fated Conjurors' Club at Whitgift) revealed – in stark terms – 'exactly' how babies were made. I was aghast! 'You do what with it?' I asked. His answer was equally uncompromising and very unlike the information we had gleaned from Twitch's biology class a couple of weeks earlier.

On that surreal occasion, I remember our glee when the bespectacled teacher with the unfortunate mannerism hesitated in the middle of bisecting a 'pregnant' frog to announce that he'd discovered something which suggested it wasn't expecting a happy (or perhaps, in the case of frogs, hoppy) event. 'Er . . . actually, it appears not to be a female of the species but a rather . . er, plump male. You see . . . Henty stop laughing immediately!'

I reckoned Colin's description of what he believed our parents frequently got up to in a bed was probably more feasible than what Twitch told us frogs got down to in a pond. Nevertheless, it came as a shock to me, and I still found it hard to believe that my own mum and dad would ever indulge in such dubious shenanigans under the sheets. As for me – well, chance would be a fine thing I suppose and anyway, the principle was all well and good, however distorted. But what about the practice? At 15 I felt a bit like the bloke in Max Miller's gag (one of many) about 'newly-weds' (from the Max Miller Appreciation Society's *Blue Book*).

'I met a pal of mine the other day. I said 'Charlie, they tell me you're married now.' He said 'That's right.' I said 'Then you'll know what's what?' He said 'What do you mean ?' I said 'If you're married, you must know what's what.' He said 'I think you're crazy.' Charlie started walking home, and as he started walking home, he kept saying to himself – Now you're married, you know what's what. When he got home that night, he got into the bedroom. The wife was in bed, so he took all his clothes off and switched the light out. He didn't want to get out again – see. He was in the dark and he was feeling around in the dark. And all of a sudden he said 'What's that?' And the wife said, 'What's what? 'ere!'

Many years later I described this nagging need to learn more about the female of the species in an article for *Mayfair* magazine which detailed my own fictional voyage into the unknown. I wrote: 'This is the hitherto unpublished account of my journey into that region – known today as Upper Thigh-Land. Now, of course, it's familiar ground: well-charted, often photographed and frequently seen on cinema and television screens. Then, in the early Fifties, it was literally virgin territory, known only to married members of the tribe, and certainly well out of bounds to the lone adventurer. As I set out on my single-minded mission, in the front room of No. 36 Montford Road, Thornton Heath, on a warm summer's evening in 1954, I remember thinking to myself – What are my chances of success? Have I chosen the right conditions? Will I make the legendary Black Hole and, if I do, will I live to tell the tale?'

Well, *Mayfair* readers were able to draw their own conclusions from what followed. It was indeed, by and large, a fictional exercise to protect the innocent – not that the young lady involved (who did exist) was all that innocent. You won't find Montford Road on a Croydon road map either, although I have to say that Thornton Heath was a happy hunting ground for the predatory Henty animal. Not for romantic reasons, you understand, but largely because it was within walking distance of Selhurst Park, London, SE25 – the home of Crystal Palace Football Club.

First team games under the newly-established floodlights made a change from two one and ninepennies – back stalls – at the ABC cinema, Broad Green. It was also important to establish whether the new girl-friend was prepared to support the Glaziers as they were known then on a regular basis. As we've already learned, my father played for Palace, as an amateur, and from a very early age, I was hooked, attending my first game (a home defeat by Norwich City) in April 1947.

No, the young lady did not necessarily have to like me but it was imperative that she was prepared to stand on a muddy terrace, knee-deep in peanut shells, and shout for the home team – 'They're the ones in the claret and blue, Barbara/Janet/Jill . . .' Oh, and a knowledge of the off-side rule was always a bonus.

Now, I know what you're thinking. No wonder he had trouble forming a 'meaningful' relationship. Well, you're wrong! Going to the game was a doddle, and there were very rarely any complaints about holding hands with me on the Holmesdale, especially on a cold night. It was when I got 'em home and standing outside the front door that my difficulties arose.

And that too! How do you kiss someone when you're wearing glasses and it's pouring with rain?

10

Attempting intimate relations on a doorstep in South London is one thing. Breaking into public relations at the age of 20 is another. Working in Peter Dowdall's service section on the eighth floor of No. 1 Kingsway was not at all how I had envisaged the business of selling an oil company to the great British public. That was the job of the photographic and film units, I soon discovered, and our job (Veronica, Maureen, Brendan and I), was to effectively 'service' their multiple needs.

I gravitated towards the photo unit, which was on another floor and consisted of four or five main photographers together with a sizeable team of darkroom technicians. I became responsible for ensuring that, when on assignment overseas or in this country, the photographers had all the correct equipment for the job and customs clearance for their valued cameras etcetera before arriving at an airport.

It was a complex business but I enjoyed it because I was interested in photography. It meant that I was out of the office quite a bit, and the photographers themselves were great characters who were easy to work for. The chief photographer was a large, ebullient man, C.D.V. (Derrick) Knight. He was rarely in the UK but when he did drop in on service section he always had a friendly word of encouragement and, indeed, suggested my name to his boss when a vacancy arose for a caption writer. Derrick knew, for example, that I had contributed several pieces to my local newspaper, the *Croydon Advertiser*, as chairman of the United Nations Association (youth section). A photograph I took of a cheerful bunch of young friends on a hike in Surrey was given prominence in the *Advertiser* on one occasion, and on another I sent back reports from Upper Austria where members of the youth section were helping refugees from the Eastern bloc to build their

My very first cartoon, which appeared in a Shell house magazine in 1957. Others followed in the BEA staff newspaper in the 60s.

own homes on land provided by the Austrian government. I enjoyed this reportage, and there will always be a certain magic about seeing ones own words in print for the first time.

Thus inspired, I leapt at the chance of 'writing for a living'. This meant moving into an office with a fellow called Robin who was similarly employed on producing the words that accompanied the photographs – not always an easy task because very often the photographers, in their haste, would supply only the minimum of background information and some of their assignments were in remote locations, thousands of miles away from these shores. Checking facts thus proved difficult at times, and it didn't help matters either to be faced with print after print of shiny pipelines and high-tech refineries which all looked alike. It was a challenge, however, and as captions are meant to be short, succinct and very much to the point, I was learning the basics of 'good journalism' with every photograph I captioned.

Despite all this progress in Shell, I still sensed the need to get away and do my own thing, and I'd not forgotten – even if he had instantly – the moment when I told Whitgift's deputy headmaster that it was my intention to make broadcasting my career. But how? The BBC then – with its Home and Light programmes – was very much a closed shop with few, if any, opportunities for newcomers to get close to a microphone. And that was it! No hospital radio. No commercial radio. No chance. Unless . . .

'What about Uncle Harry in California ?' I asked my incredulous father one evening after we'd both returned – Shell-shocked as usual – on the 6.04.

'What about him?' he said cautiously.

'Well, I have met Harry – and Aunt Ella – when they were last over here. Do you think they'd accommodate me in Santa Barbara for a time so I could get some radio experience in the States?'

Silence. This was not the path Henty senior had planned for his only son to follow. In fact, to him it was tantamount to my saying, 'I think I'd like to be the first man on the moon dad.'

To be fair, he did provide me with Harry's address and I wrote a letter explaining my situation and asking whether he and his wife would be prepared to 'sponsor' me in my emigration bid and provide me with accommodation upon my arrival on the west coast. And yes, I did say 'emigrate'. A giant step.

Harry East was very much a self-made man who was born in this country, married one of my grandmother's sisters, Ella, in Oxford and moved to America in the 1930s to further his horse-riding ambitions. He and his wife eventually ended up on the west coast because diminutive Harry had become an international polo player of repute and most of the serious clubs were based in California.

Serious in money terms, that is. My distant relative had given up playing the game and was employed by the exclusive Santa Barbara Polo Club as a coach. Apparently he lived in the foothills of Montecito, just above the city, in modest accommodation probably provided by the club. He spoke well of life in America and painted for me a vivid picture of white, Spanish-style buildings, perfect weather, oranges growing on the trees year-round, and – in Santa Barbara alone – at least four local radio stations. Perhaps his description was too vivid, but it certainly impressed me as the rain bucketted down in our South Croydon back garden.

California in the late 1950s was still on another planet to most British people – Planet Hollywood, if you like, because that was the only way the majority of us could imagine this faraway Never Never Land. No Virgin Atlantic then. No 15-day tours from LA to San Francisco with a couple of nights in Las Vegas thrown in. California was, by and large, a no-go area for UK citizens in 1959, and that made me even more determined to get there and, hopefully, stay there. California Here I Come! Or do I?

In his reply to my letter, Harry said he would be happy to welcome me to Santa Barbara but warned that finding employment of any sort would not be at all easy and this was a requirement if he was to sponsor me. He said the radio stations were mostly operated by very small broadcasting teams. One of them was run by a husband with the help of his wife, another was closely associated with the city's daily newspaper, the *Santa Barbara News Press*. Harry strongly recommended that I should get some journalistic experience under my belt as a matter of priority and, naturally, I needed no further prompting.

I rang the editor of the *Croydon Advertiser* within hours of receiving the airmail letter, and within a couple of weeks Bob Taylor had offered me the opportunity to work as a trainee reporter at No. 36 High Street, Croydon, for the princely sum of – wait for it – three pounds a week. Don't believe me? Neither did my faint-hearted father, but here's the diary entry for Monday, 25th May, 1959: 'Mr. Taylor of the *Advertiser* rang early in the morning and confirmed Saturday's offer – £3 a week for 3 months. This is probably it!'

The three months from the beginning of September was a direct reference to the fact that I still intended to depart these shores for America, regardless, at the beginning of 1960. The editor was aware of this but happy to take me on for what we both saw as a 'trial period'. To me it was a golden opportunity. To my father, it was a dangerous step into the unknown. He said very little, but dad was a worrier and I know that it troubled him a lot.

Within months he suffered a heart-attack while at the dreaded Shell Court, and I will always be conscious of the fact that my dramatic decision may have caused this crisis in his life. Dad survived the attack though, and lived to realise that – despite his misgivings – I had made the right decision to leave Shell. And that was the unanimous verdict of all my PR colleagues at No. 1 Kingsway too when I told them the news.

They were less than impressed by the weekly salary I was being offered – 'How much?' – but overall I sensed they were envious of my plans. I left on the final day of July and observed in the diary: 'A big step John Henty and we hope in the right direction. Everyone was very nice and I bought mum some flowers in Croydon.'

In 1958, working for Shell public relations at No. 1 Kingsway in London, I was strongly influenced by the popular Goon Show. A touch of the Bentines here, I suspect.

11

Oddly enough, flowers played a prominent part in the first few weeks of my journalistic training, and I'm not referring to the excellent bitter beer bearing that name which was on tap at Batty's Bar just across the road from the *Advertiser* offices. More often than not, the reporters would adjourn to the Express Cafe in the high street, where copious cups of tea and coffee were consumed along with sticky Belgian buns and (a lifetime favourite of mine) sugary Eccles cakes.

No, the flowers that I became deeply involved with in the early days of September were the winning blooms in numerous autumn flower shows at church halls right across the borough of Croydon and beyond. One of my jobs, alongside the weddings and petrol station openings, was to telephone the horticultural society secretaries after an event to get a quote for the opening paragraph and then a full (and I mean full) list of all the winners. There were hundreds of 'em, and all the various classes had to be included, using the unique newspaper style for words like dahlia, chrysanthemum and fuchsia. Then there were Bill Goddard's photographs of the winning gardeners to caption, plus chase-up calls to the secretaries who were never in. It was demanding but, again, I enjoyed the buzz of working in a busy office, and I did get out on various innocent assignments from time to time.

In the reporters' room on the third floor front I came in for a certain amount of gentle ribbing because of the fact that I had been educated at Whitgift, the local public school. At that time it was almost unheard of for someone from those hallowed halls to demean themselves by working in journalism. As usual, John Henty was very happy to be the exception to the rule, but I still felt it was sad that so much emphasis at my school had been placed on the professions – the City, banking, insurance and the like.

Our chief reporter was a journalist from the old school, Harold Snelling, a charming, rather eccentric man who told us he went swimming every day and was for ever cutting up windfall apples from his garden with an ancient penknife. Among other things, Harold was responsible for detailing 'jobs' from the daily diary of events which sat on his cluttered desk.

The crime reporter, David Barber, had his own schedule, regularly checking the police stations and covering the magistrates court cases across the region. Dave was never happier than when he had a 'decent' murder to get his teeth into but, unlike today in south London, violent crime was a relatively rare occurrence then.

The office junior was a young man who later in life went into comedy script-writing for the BBC and, more recently, was heavily involved in Thames Television's 'This Is Your Life' programme. In the early winter of 1959 Joe Steeples was very good at making cups of tea for reporters who were either too busy or too lazy to cross the road to the Express cafe. This task he accomplished in a room at the top of the building where the newspaper archives were kept, and one afternoon, the half-empty contents of a cold pot of tea (no tea bags then) were surreptitiously slung out of a window into the high street below. Management was not amused but it certainly tickled the fancy of the reporters' room and I soon established a rapport with the rebellious tea-maker from Waddon. Later, we were to work together on the *Beckenham and Penge Advertiser*.

Yes, unbeknown to us, the 'big time' was just around the corner, but first, for me, there was America to conquer and all the formalities involved in getting a visa and the right sponsorship forms back from Uncle Harry in Santa Barbara. And how was I going to get there? After all, £3 a week (with an extra 15 shillings for Sunday jobs) was not going to stretch to 8,000 miles of air travel, even in 1960.

I consulted a school chum, Dick Tucker, who had also chosen not to become 'something in the city' on leaving Whitgift. He was running a successful travel agency and advised me to fly economy to New York and then take a Greyhound bus for the onward journey to California.

'It's cheap. You'll actually see America and meet lots of interesting people,' he enthused.

This sounded fine. I discussed the details at home, and within a couple of days, I was the owner of a PanAm ticket for a Boeing 707 flight from Heathrow to Idlewild Airport, New York, on Wednesday, 20th January, 1960. ONE-WAY! This was it John . . . and there was literally no going back. Or perhaps?

Oh dear! You see, being a 'newspaper reporter' appeared to have given my persona a new zip and, ironically enough, at a time when I was about to 'leave these shores' forever, female company became much less of a problem and one girl in particular, Julie, endeared herself to me, to such an extent that I even debated whether I should go at all. Typical – bloody typical.

Mind you, whether Miss D. felt exactly the same way about this cub reporter is an entirely different matter. Shakespeare may have written frequently about unrequited love: John Henty had got it down to a fine art – ask Rosemary, Barbara, Janet, Ann, Diane, Norma. . .

So I bought myself a Revelation suitcase, wrote my initials on it, put a black and white film in my camera, wound up mum and dad's present (a travelling alarm clock) and prepared for what promised to be a Great Adventure, a journey into the unknown – and it was just that, because my only other experience of travel abroad, apart from the refugee camps of Upper Austria, had been an organised school trip to Lake Como in the summer of 1952.

I reflected on this as I flew at 31,000 feet above the barren wastes of Greenland on that January morning. I ordered myself a Rye Highball and wrote prophetically in my diary: 'From now, it is impossible to record all events fully.' I noted a 'much clearer atmosphere' upon arrival and added: 'Would someone please pinch me!'

In New York I stayed with two school friends on the West Side at 344 W88th Street and spent the first few days acclimatising myself to a very, very different way of life. Tony and Pat had both found themselves jobs, so I played tourist during the day and made a visit to an old friend of my father's, Billy Dalton, who lived with his wife at Mount Vernon. I also went to a cinema just off Time Square where I saw the first-ever movie featuring 'Aromarama', or 'smelly-vision' if you like – a bizarre concept which involved pumping different odours into the half-empty theatre (odourtorium?) which were then identified by captions on the giant screen. The film was called 'Behind The Great Wall' and was basically a run-of-the-mill travel documentary with a gimmick. The fault with the gimmick was that the smells were largely unfamiliar to Western noses. I mean, when was the last time you got a whiff of a Manchurian tigress? Or sniffed a cordite bomb? Exactly! And it didn't help matters either, towards the end, when the pumping system failed to extract the pongs and we were shrouded in an evil-smelling haze.

Never mind, it made a good piece for the *Advertiser* and was the first of several articles I wrote during my journey across America. So that's where Bill Bryson got the idea . . .

12

The journey itself started at the Greyhound Bus Terminal in New York when I climbed aboard the Chicago Express at 6 pm for an overnight ride on the vast intercity turnpikes that criss-cross the Eastern States. And remember, up until that Monday evening I had never before seen a motorway, or a launderette or a help-yourself supermarket or restaurant, and I'd certainly never experienced the openness with which I was greeted, time and again, by fellow passengers.

At first I found it almost intrusive, but by the time we'd moved on from Chicago (where I stayed in the YMCA) and were powering through Omaha, North Platte and 'cowboy country', I soon lost my British reserve and was swapping family details with the best of 'em.

'Hi, I'm John – a journalist – and I come from Croydon in England. How are you?'

One fellow passenger was even more forthcoming though, and that was on the section out of Salt Lake City bound for my final destination, San Francisco. I'd enjoyed a beautiful day in the Mormon city, and visited the remarkable temple and the capitol building for the State of Utah. The coach was crowded. I turned up late and there was only one gangway seat on the upper section of the bus which I preferred.

Tired from all my walking about, I slumped into the vacant seat without giving any thought as to who I was sitting next to. I think I was vaguely aware of the fact that my fellow passenger was female but we certainly did not exchange any of the usual passing pleasantries.

The mighty vehicle roared off into the night and fairly soon the main lights were dimmed, seats were adjusted to allow some sort of sleep and I closed my eyes and dozed fitfully. Apparently my companion had no such problem. Perhaps she was more of a seasoned traveller, but within minutes she was fast asleep and, as so often happens when sitting upright and travelling, her head lolled, first to the right, and then to the left – ending up on my shoulder. By accident?

It stayed there, and I suddenly thought to myself: this is nice. I don't believe Sinatra had recorded 'Strangers In The Night' by January 1960, but if he had, no doubt I'd have started humming it. I also noticed that the hair was blonde, the owner was slightly older than myself and seemed to be quite content – in fact, very content to be nestling on my shoulder.

Well now, what next?

I'll tell you what, dear anxious reader. Without any compunction, I turned my head and gently kissed her on the forehead. That's what. Foreplay? Forget it: this was pure instinct, and she immediately responded by snuggling even closer to me. Of course, Martha (for that was her name) could have 'awoken' screaming and claiming that she'd been assaulted. That was a risk I suppose that I took. What is remarkable though is the fact that we'd not spoken one word to each other and yet, through the night, shared an intimacy and togetherness under the standard-issue Greyhound blankets that I still marvel at today.

The next morning Martha told me that she was from Switzerland and travelling to take-up work as an au pair in San Francisco. Happily, we both accepted that we were lonely people a long way from home and somehow, for a brief moment in time, had found comfort in each others company. There was an innocence about it which I really don't think you would be able to achieve today. Certainly not on a Greyhound bus. In San Francisco, on that final Saturday in January 1960, we parted, never to see each other again.

There were new friends to meet though, and as Martha headed off to find her host family I was greeted by a girl whom I had last seen as we dug a cesspit together in Lambach, Upper Austria, 18 months previously. How about that for a romantic setting? Kathy Yarwood's family lived in Berkeley, just outside San Francisco, and she and two of her sisters were waiting at the terminal to pick up the dishevelled and ever-so-slightly disorientated English bloke.

I was whisked away by sisters three in what I described later in my diary as a 'massive' car. To me, all cars in America were enormous – especially if you compared them with my old banger (a Morris 12) back home in Croydon. Once installed with the Yarwood family on Oxford Street, Berkeley, I enjoyed a shower, a meal and a rest before (and this was to be typical of my new life on the west coast) they rushed me back into the city to act as an unpaid usher at the Geary Theatre for a performance of 'The Pleasure Of His Company'.

Apparently, the theatre used students to help out in the auditorium before and during a presentation, and my job was to show people to their seats. This turned out to be hilarious because, clearly, I had no concept of the large theatre's layout and consequently my parties were taken on lengthy tours of the circle area before finding their correct seats. I was also identified as an Englishman – clearly out of his depth – and this caused even more amusement among the sophisticated Saturday evening theatre-goers. On stage, the star of the show, Rupert Everitt, was an Englishman. In the circle, there was another English eccentric: John Henty. I enjoyed his performance. He knew nothing about mine – hopefully.

My plan was to move on to Santa Barbara after spending a week in the Golden Gate city, and what a week it proved to be We dined out in China Town, where I learned to use chopsticks for the first time. We spent a day north of the city at Tomales Bay, hiring a boat and rowing across the bay for a picnic lunch on the beach (It's February, I kept reminding myself) and we did all the tourist things from the Japanese tea gardens to the famous Fisherman's Wharf. I even bought some poetry and a tin whistle in the 'beatnik' end of town where my beard – grown in Austria – was welcomed by the guys hanging out on 'Beach'.

'Hey, cool man!'

Unfortunately, the same modest growth was not to be appreciated by my ultra-conservative uncle down the coast in Santa Barbara, my next destination.

13

The Greyhound bus – using the spectacular Highway 101 – took just over eight hours to reach the outskirts of Santa Barbara. It was foggy as we pulled to a halt in the modest terminal building at 9 o'clock in the evening but I immediately spotted Harry and Ella as they scurried across to greet me. Somehow they were older than I had expected – almost frail in a sense – but their embrace was strong enough, and they guided me towards Harry's rather ancient vehicle, parked in the street opposite.

The journey up to Montecito in the foothills of the Santa Ynez mountains was, shall we say, not without its moments. The fog was still hanging around mysteriously and Harry, being rather short, could just about see over the sizeable steering wheel.

'We don't normally drive at night,' Aunt Ella remarked, as we lurched our way through the city streets.

I'm not entirely surprised, I thought to myself.

Their home on Buena Vista Road – rather like their physical appearance – was not quite what I had imagined when writing those lengthy letters from Croydon the year before. Many of the properties in Montecito were owned by extremely wealthy people with large grounds, swimming pools and even personal security guards. Harry and Ella's wooden abode was more shack than hacienda. However, it suited their purposes and was close-by the polo club where Harry continued to act as coach. In fact, he is still remembered there today, with the annual Harry East memorial cup.

On that first evening I suppose we both sized each other up over a welcome cup of tea, and my uncle's conclusion was, rather alarmingly, that the beard would have to go. It represented to him, intrinsically, the much-hated hippy heritage and there was no way that he was going to introduce me to his polo-playing pals wearing a beard. No way! On another occasion Harry became convinced that I was a friend of Russia and accused me of being a 'Goddam Commie!' And remember, it was around this time that McCarthyism was rife in the USA. I'm just lucky he didn't have me deported on that very first night. But what to do about the beard? As far as Mr. East was concerned, it was very much a case of 'Hair today but it better be gone tomorrow!'

The following day, a Sunday, Harry and Ella were due at the club for the first match in the Harry East Cup and of course I was invited to join them – as the long-lost 'nephew' from the Old Country, but on one condition so . . . after reading a letter from Julie which awaited my arrival (and cheered me up), I decided, with mixed-feelings, to shave off the beard. After all, I could always grow it again, and I realised only too well that finding a job of any sort was not going to be easy in Santa Barbara and what I needed, above all else, were contacts. The sort of people who might spend a leisurely afternoon out at the polo-fields, south of the city, perhaps?

That was the theory. In reality, most of the 'beautiful' people we met that rather dull afternoon were either Argentinian, extremely bored or recently retired and filthy-rich – in some cases, all at the same time. They appreciated Harry for his ability to teach them their specialised sport. They tolerated me – without the beard – because I was with him. Oh, they were pleasant enough in a 'Have a nice day' sort of way, but in terms of 'Have a nice job – ring this number on Monday', I soon realised that I would need to get downtown promptly myself and meet some real people.

Harry, of course, didn't understand this but did suggest that I should take some driving lessons to obtain my California licence, which would give me an added and essential job qualification. What sort of job really didn't bother me, because my plan was to spend as much time as I could learning about small-town radio. Right from the outset it had been made clear to me that employment with a local station was not an option as they were bound by strict regulations laid-down by the Federal Communication Commission (FCC). This decreed that only American citizens could be employed in a working capacity. However, I soon discovered that all the stations were willing to give me practical, unpaid experience on a part-time basis.

This meant that in the next two to three months, I was to be heard on K.I.S.T Radio reading the world news occasionally, and on ultra-zany station K.A.C.Y at Port Hueneme extolling the 'virtues' of Chuck's Motorola and TV Company on State Street – in a very posh, over-the-top English voice. They loved it and for a time I suppose I was the local version of Robert Morley or perhaps Laurence Olivier.

Even switchboard operators asked me to repeat things for them, and I remember thinking that my own telephone operator mum would have been very proud of her well-spoken son. Much as I enjoyed the experience – and the whole concept of 24-hour radio appealed to me enormously – it was not a proper job, and in the first couple of weeks in Santa Barbara I dashed around the city, chasing work with increasing desperation.

Al is a pal

For his part, Harry set me up with a wealthy French widow in Montecito who, he said, was seeking a chauffeur to ferry her up and down the west coast. Magnificent house, maid answered the door, but the widow, on seeing me, answered along the lines of: 'Certainment non!' A chauffeur without a valid licence did have limited potential, I guess, and perhaps, the lady of luxury had other duties in mind for her 'handy-man'?

In the city I made contact with a charitable organisation, the Direct Relief Foundation, which aimed to raise money and provide aid for third world countries. Unfortunately, I did not qualify as a third world country (almost, but not quite) and, in addition, there was an awkward misunderstanding of my personal status in the States. They assumed that because I had a Montecito address I was self-supporting and not in need of funds. In fact, they probably thought I was exceedingly rich.

When I pointed out to the manager that this was not the case, his attitude towards me cooled considerably and I have to say that his change in approach was not untypical. If there is one aspect of American life which, even today, I find depressing it is the insincerity of it all. If only I could believe that the breakfast waitress really wanted me to 'have a nice day' or was truly interested in my well-being with 'Hi, how are you?' The superficiality of 'friendship' was so obvious to me in my hesitant state and I soon recognised my novelty value at dinner parties and chamber of commerce meetings.

On the other hand, there were those who were genuinely concerned for my well-being. One freelance writer in particular, a guy called Al Stump – who was 'big' on baseball – came to my rescue when he heard of my treatment by the not quite so charitable organisation on Haley Street. By this time, I had found myself accommodation in the city centre, at the rear of what was the Oxford Bookshop at 1215 Anacapa Street.

The 50 dollars a month rent needed paying. My initial funds were running low and there was no way I was going to cable home to seek financial help from dad. There were no e-mails then remember and, sadly, it took two weeks for me to learn, by airmail letter from mum, that the poor fellow had suffered a heart attack at the dreaded Shell Court on a Monday morning at the beginning of February.

Typically, mum may have chosen to delay forwarding bad news, but at least she was able to add that he was 'greatly improved now' and 'making a speedy recovery'. However, at a distance of eight thousand miles I was still upset by her letter and it didn't help to have the prospect of a job taken away from me by an organisation that should have behaved better.

I'd met Al over an iced coffee in the courtyard of the El Paseo restaurant – a delightful, shaded terrace, surrounded by orange trees with real oranges growing in February. I told him of my predicament and the hopes that I had of working part-time, in radio while earning some money with the Direct Relief Foundation. I mentioned that they had reneged on the deal when it became clear that I was not the long-lost son of William Hearst.

Al was not amused. That night he invited me back to his place, where his charming wife cooked me an enormous steak and Mr Stump plied me with copious drams of his finest malt whiskey. I slept very well that night in my new apartment – unworried by anything – and the very next morning, unbeknown to me, Al picked up the phone and spoke strongly to the Foundation supremo. As a direct result of this – over lunch in the Copper Coffee Pot –- I was offered paid temporary employment at $1.50 an hour in the charity's main office, on the understanding that I would actively seek paid work elsewhere by enrolling with a private employment agency.

Meantime, miraculously, I had passed my California driving test with a 100 per cent rating. So things were looking up, and I decided that there was no need for me to re-visit the local job centre where I had actually stood in line with a bunch of migrant Mexicans seeking work as lemon-pickers. Believe me, that was a low point and I shall always remember the spontaneous friendship of a guy called Al.

14

Within a couple of days, and following a couple of fairly probing interviews set-up by a local agency, I was offered an office job with the Title Insurance and Trust Company on East Figueroa. Although it meant absolutely nothing to me, I was proudly told that I would be joining the largest title company in the world. So that was all right, then.

My job in the (oh, not again) open-plan office of the single storey building was to keep on top of the filing, organise the post, both inwards and outwards, and make two daily runs through the city, servicing banks, the county court house and other financial institutions. The 'titles' related to land and, as far as I could ascertain, our job was to establish ownership of that land in and around the city – much of which had originally been owned by Spanish settlers.

Historically, it was fascinating stuff and the bonus for me was that my small apartment was only a couple of blocks away – a five minute walk down Anacapa. It soon became very familiar territory, and I was able to establish a regular routine with breakfast in Stan's Breakfast House and more often than not, dinner in the Copper Coffee Pot. There were cinemas too, and the Lobero Theatre for stage presentations, and I even made contact with a bunch of ex-pat British guys who had formed a cricket team with away fixtures up and down the west coast.

They played mostly at home though, and this was because the Santa Barbara teas were just like those 'back-home' and everyone wanted to sample the dainty sandwiches, Scotch pancakes, fruit cake and mugs of real tea produced – unbelievably – from an ancient tea-urn. The catering was provided by a man and his wife who were in service with one of those Montecito millionaires.

They did it in style, and while our cricket was not of a high standard, the teas were the toast of the coast. Visiting Americans just could not believe that we'd invented a sport where you played fairly leisurely with bat and ball for a couple of hours, then stopped to consume an enormous amount of food, before proceeding with what for them was the 'second period' – and this while dressed in all-white gear with the occasional peculiar attachment and raucous shouts of ''Owzat?'

'How's *what*?' demanded one Highway Patrol cop who was watching from the edge of the field.

I tried to explain, fearful that we were about to be 'busted' for un-American activities.

My biggest problem was transport. Passing a driving test is one thing but having sufficient funds to purchase a reasonable car, even in America, was another. I had to rely very heavily on the friends I was beginning to make at T.I. (Title Insurance). They included a pleasant guy from the north-east of England, Ron Blakey, whose parents operated a mobile home centre just out of town, and a young Californian whose family originated from Denmark, Phil Westergaard.

Santa Barbara, California, in 1960. A new typewriter, a new face, a job and a drive in Phil Westergaard's Austin Healey Sprite.

They both had cars. In fact, Phil, when I first met him, owned three vehicles: an old Buick which had a baseball club for a gear lever, a sporting Austin Healey Sprite and the *pièce de résistance* as far as I was concerned, an enormous Chevrolet Impala. It was in the Chevvy that Phil and I travelled down the coast to Hollywood on St. George's Day – a Saturday – in 1960. We did some shopping in Beverley Hills and then cruised Hollywood and Vine in a vain search for any sort of celebrity. I would have favoured a glimpse of the actress/dancer Vera Ellen or perhaps a camp cameo from the great Alfred Hitchcock himself but that, amazingly enough, was to come later for Phil and me – and not in L.A.

I shall always recall the journey back to Santa Barbara on the 101 that Saturday evening. The record on the radio was Vic Damone singing 'Never Will I Marry. At one point a whole herd of wild horses dashed across the freeway some distance in front of us, to be caught in our headlights. Throughout, I kept reminding myself that this really was happening to me. I'd been to Hollywood, I was living in America and England seemed a very, very long way away that night.

Was I homesick ? In a sense, yes. I did miss the quirky British sense of humour (frequently playing tapes I'd made in the UK of the Goon Shows to anyone who would listen). The response was almost always the same: baffled bemusement. When Peter Sellers made a brief appearance on the coast-to-coast Jack Paar TV Show, I wrote to him, care of the BBC, and was astonished to get a hand-written reply from the man himself within two or three weeks of writing. I still have the letter today. Peter spoke of the weather in Hertfordshire where he was living at the time. He added – and I believe he did have psychic abilities – 'You sound homesick, old man. Why not come home? It's beautiful here at the moment . . .'

Then there were Kennedy's sausages from Crown Hill in Croydon. I frequently lusted after them in Stan's Breakfast House, where pancakes were fine but Oh, for a banger, sizzling and ripe! Then what about rain, fog, Crystal Palace football club and, of course, Julie.

She may not have been missing me but I would have welcomed her gentle company for visits to the cinema and walks down to the beach area. Not having a car also meant that I was in an impossible situation when it came to attempting a date. The bus service in the city, even then, was quixotic and trains were non-existent unless you were heading either up or down the coast.

What California Girl was going to go out with a Croydon Boy anyway if she had to pick him up from his place in her car? Drive-in cinemas were all the rage around this time as well, and afforded plenty of opportunities for getting to know that special person . . . if you had wheels. I had to make do with solo visits to the Fox Arlington and State cinemas downtown. I even saw 'Carry On Nurse' there on one occasion.

On St. Patrick's Day, Ron Blakey – who did have a girl friend – invited me to join them for a visit to the Fiesta Bowl, a ten-pin bowling establishment on the outskirts of the city. I'd never been bowling and as far as I knew there were no such centres anywhere in the United Kingdom. That casual visit was a revelation to me. I was enormously impressed by the layout of the place, how busy it was on a Thursday evening, the mix of men and women playing and the overall sense of communal enjoyment.

Young or old, everyone seemed to be entering into the spirit of the place. I even had a go and was exhilarated to achieve a couple of 'strikes' during the evening (all the pins knocked down with one ball) despite never having played the game before. I'd go so far as to say it was addictive, and the next day I mentioned my enthusiasm to one or two of the guys on the open floor at T.I. I added that I thought it would be massively popular in my own home town of Croydon.

'How many Bowls do you have there at the moment ?' Phil asked me. When I said that, to the best of my knowledge, there were no bowling establishments in the entire country the statement was greeted with mass incredulity. 'None?' they all cried. At this juncture, I should point out that the same guys were equally amazed when I said that there was no local radio in the UK and, by and large, we only enjoyed three flavours of icecream – vanilla, strawberry and chocolate.

'You mean you have no pistachio, no chocolate chip, no English toffee? How do you survive?' I began to wonder myself, and when Phil and I discussed the matter back at his apartment, we agreed that here was a business opportunity waiting to be exploited. By *us.* Oh dear!

15

I'm afraid it's true that I do have an unsettling effect on people. At Shell we were all planning a mass escape from the Hounsditch Penitentiary. Even at the *Croydon Advertiser* in three short months, my immigration plans had caused a degree of unrest amongst those trapped in Penge or banged-up in Banstead. In the spring of 1960 Phil Westergaard was doing very nicely, thank you, at the Title Insurance and Trust Company. He'd never heard of a place called Croydon. He had a delightful all-American girfriend, Caroline, who loved him dearly and Phil was a leading light in the Santa Barbara Junior Chamber of Commerce.

So why throw all this up to join an eccentric, penniless Englishman on a speculative venture 8,000 miles away from southern California? Well, you'll have to ask Phil that question, and here's his telephone number . . . No, seriously, he still lives in California today with his charming second wife, Rosalie, and still communicates with me on a regular basis and we've met on more than one occasion in the UK and quite recently on the west coast.

I'm sure Phil will tell you that we did what we did because of a genuine belief in the project. After our initial discussion, Phil spoke with US business contacts of his in the bowling business. We travelled down to Los Angeles and met with representatives of the Brunswick organisation (a major player in the US ten-pin bowling business) and they were very encouraging. The game was going to take-off in the UK, Croydon was an ideal location for a bowling centre and we would be in at the start.

The only thing that was not mentioned on our first visit to LA was . . . money. Phil and his friend Henry were confident that money would be forthcoming if the idea was good enough. And they reckoned it was. For my part, I sounded out contacts in Croydon by letter and even raised the matter with my father who had, by now, taken early retirement from Shell. All UK parties were uniformly cautious in their replies, but that did not really surprise me. It only served to underline the enormous difference between southern California and South Croydon when it came to innovative business.

It also explained why, in 1960, most of us only enjoyed three flavours of icecream in the UK, had one monolithic broadcasting organisation for the whole country and no ten-pin bowling centres, although one was planned for Golders Green in London. There was little I could do about the ice cream (although I was tempted), and the BBC would need seven more years to get round to local radio, but bowling was a different matter. Phil, Henry and I decided to make a go of it, and the first requirement was to get over to England, find a suitable site and then raise the necessary money.

If only life was that simple, but hey – we were young, enthusiastic and Phil was prepared to stump up the air fare for the two of us. Henry would remain state-side and gee things up with Brunswick in Los Angeles, 'awaiting our numerous calls'. Meantime, I carried on working for T.I. on East Figuero and Phil prepared to drop his bombshell at home in Ventura where girlfriend Caroline was not going to be amused by the dramatic news: 'I'm leaving for a foreign shore with an Englishman I've only just met!'

Imagine! I handed in my notice at the end of June, had a farewell drink with Al Stump in the El Paseo and drove, with Phil, up to Montecito where Harry and Ella were philosophical about our plans.

I wrote in my diary: 'I said 'au revoir' to Uncle and Aunt for a while. Uncle still a very great incentive (sic)' and so he was – fully supportive of my endeavours, despite the fact that at one stage he had regarded me as a dangerous subversive – a view no doubt shared right now by the beautiful Caroline, who made the most of her time left with Phil by joining us wherever we went. This included the local drive-in cinema where I enjoyed watching my hero Peter Sellers in 'The Mouse That Roared' from the front seat of the '37 Buick while my companions in the back pretended I wasn't there. Talk about a gooseberry.

Our TWA Polar flight to London via San Francisco was scheduled for the day after Independence Day. Phil had sold his faithful Buick on 4th July for $25 and I'd rung Aunt Ella for a final chat. The flight departed Los Angeles at 9.30 on the Tuesday morning, and after an uneventful couple of hours flying up the coast, we arrived in San Francisco where passengers were allowed off the aircraft while others joined for the overnight journey to London. Phil and I decided to stretch our legs and moved into the enormous transit lounge for a coffee and an opportunity to make one or two last minute phone calls. I rang the Yarwood family in Berkeley, and Phil? He spoke with Caroline.

Once this had been accomplished we just sat and viewed our fellow passengers. Imagine my amazement when I noticed a very familiar, portly figure slowly walking across the wide expanse of floor – with a small white dog under each arm. It couldn't be. Surely not. Never in a million years . . . And yet, it was. Indeed it was - the film director Alfred Hitchcock, making a public appearance just as though he were acting – ever so briefly – in one of his own distinctive movies.

Mr. Hitchcock was not bound for London I subsequently discovered and had only recently completed filming 'Vertigo', starring Kim Novak, in his beloved northern California. The dogs were Sealyham Terriers, a Welsh breed very popular in Hollywood during the 20s and 30s. Stars like Gary Cooper, Cary Grant Humphrey Bogart and our own Welshman, Richard Burton, owned Sealyhams, and two of them even made an appearance with Hitchcock in his next movie, 'The Birds', in 1963.

However, in San Francisco they provided the great man with a perfect excuse for not signing an autograph for me. I politely made my approach – emphasizing that I came from England – and that I was a fan of his. What else? Mr H. declined graciously, pointing out that a dog under each arm made writing rather difficult. He moved on in determined fashion and I returned to Phil, who had witnessed the unlikely confrontation.

Funnily enough, my life has been full of such fragmentary meetings – brief encounters if you like – and I think now's a good time to indulge in a little unashamed name-dropping' while Phil and I travel over the Pole and through the night . . .

16

Yes, for a whole range of highly obscure reasons, I've had my fair share of encounters with well-known people over the years. Celebrities we like to call 'em now – individuals who have made some impact on this wobbly old world of ours by lifting their lives out of the mundane and into the extraordinary. With one or two notable (and they shall remain unnamed) exceptions, I have always found these characters (for that is what they are) approachable.

Oh, sometimes, there was a pernickety PR person who tried to do their jobsworth bit, but in the main – well, let me give you an example. Hollywood legend Charlton Heston was appearing at our local theatre in a demanding role which required his presence on stage for most of the play. Surely there was no way he would find time to be interviewed, however briefly, for, of all things, national hospital radio. Wrong! I left a note for him in advance with the stage door, and you can imagine my surprise – and delight – when I got a call from the company PA to say 'Yes, Mr. Heston would be happy to see you on Thursday between the matinee and evening performance'.

On the day I was shown into his small dressing room – and it may have been the size of the room that somehow emphasised what a powerful-looking guy was this star of 'Ben Hur', 'Planet of the Apes' etcetera. He was no longer a young man, of course, but Charlton Heston had presence, and he could not have been more accommodating during our brief get-together.

To achieve a decent sound balance for my tape recorder, we shared a back-stage sofa which had definitely seen better days. I have to admit to being a trifle over-awed on this occasion and, after all, what do you ask a legend when you've only got 10 minutes at the most to do it in. It's all very well for the Michael Parkinsons of this world and their relay of researchers, but my two or three questions were going to be crucial.

So I tried to be original – and it worked. No, I did not say, as one colleague suggested, 'How did it all start for you, Chuck?' What I did ask was: 'Mr. Heston, you must have been interviewed hundreds of times before. Have you ever been an interviewer yourself?'

Now, of course, if the answer had been 'Well, no, actually!' then I was in trouble. As it happened, Mr H. had indeed conducted some interviews on behalf of the BBC several years back, and as a self-confessed Anglophile he enjoyed the experience and was happy to tell me all about it. From that point, on we were in business, and I was even able to throw in one brief reference to 'that' chariot race.

Another Hollywood legend - but for an entirely different reason - was the great Mel Blanc who provided the voices for, amongst others, Tweetie Pie, Porky Pig, Speedy Gonzales and my all-time cartoon favourite, the ebullient Bugs Bunny.

As a 'voice' man myself (I even advertised in the *Stage* newspaper, using a photograph and caption which read: 'Not to be taken at face value alone – for the VOICE of your CHOICE – contact . . .') Mel Blanc was a hero

of mine, no question about it – and I spent many happy hours in those wonderful cartoon cinemas in Sixties London watching Bugs, the Road Runner, Daffy Duck and Sylvester The Cat, and listening to 'the Master's' versatile voice.

I even wrote to Warner Brothers in Hollywood and suggested that I would like to interview the man. The studio replied casually, and pre-dictably: 'Mr. Henty, if you're ever in Los Angeles we'll see what we can do for you. In the meantime, thank you for your interest in Warner Brothers cartoons . . .'. What they didn't know – and what you will soon be discovering – is that I was working for an airline at the time, and within weeks of receiving their letter I was on the telephone to the studio from a call box in downtown LA.

To be fair, they remembered my request but pointed out that as Mr. Blanc was a freelance artist I would have to ring him myself to set up the interview. This I did, and who should answer the phone but the unmistakeable voice of the man himself. He gave me directions. I boarded a bus and within an hour I was sitting in a modest office overlooking the junction of Hollywood and Vine.

Mel had recently suffered a horrendous road accident and was being eased back into the job by his son, who stayed in the room all the time. The interview was a dream come true for me, and it was so easy. All I had to do really was switch on the tape recorder and sit there. The famous voices came pouring out of the tiny, dynamic man and he spoke of his friendship with the British radio personality, Sam Costa. It was Sam, as DJ, who gave Mel a big hit in the UK charts in 1950 with 'I Tawt I Taw A Puddy Tat!'

On my return, the interview was broadcast on the BBC Home Service in a programme, produced by Bobby Jaye, devoted to the movie-going public. I kept in touch with Mel by letter, and was sad to learn of his death in 1989 when they claim his final words were 'That's All Folks!' No, I don't believe it either! Nor the rumour that the guy who created the voice of Bugs Bunny was allergic . . . to carrots.

Catch-phrases were very much a part of Mel Blanc's lively life, and he even signed his business card for me (*previous page*) with the words 'What's up, Doc?' Tommy Cooper, of course, was besieged wherever he went by people expecting to come face-to-fez with a giant of a man uttering the immortal words 'Just like that!' Not in my case. It was 1983. Tommy had been booked by a major Croydon department store to open some exhibition or other, and I was engaged to keep the crowd happy

I met the man behind the voice of Bugs Bunny, Mel Blanc, in his Hollywood office on March 12, 1964, when this photo was taken.

while awaiting his arrival, introducing him to everybody with a big-booster build-up.

Tommy ambled in ever-so-slightly late – sans fez, wearing a rather crumpled suit and carrying a half-open holdall. I thought he looked a tired man but the cheers of the small crowd bucked him up no end and soon he was cracking the odd silly gag or two and, yes, throwing in the occasional 'Just like that!'. They loved it, but my impression was that it was all a bit of an effort. Tommy Cooper was feeling world-weary.

After the opening we retired to the store's managerial offices where a splendid buffet lunch, with drinks, had been prepared. Imagine the surprise of the assembled directors when Tommy rustled about in his holdall and produced a pack of sandwiches and a small can of non-alcoholic lager. He explained, rather sheepishly, that he was on some sort of diet and was only following doctor's instructions. Then, as if to make up for what he saw as a *faux pas*, he again delved into the magic holdall and pulled out a packaged conjuring trick – the sort of novelty item to be found on sale in 'fun' shops across the country. And yes, he had bought it himself (possibly on a recent visit to the Blackpool pleasure beach area) and was clearly amused by it in almost a child-like way.

Others have confirmed that Tommy was always buying commercially-made tricks for his own divertissement. What puzzled me was the fact that he obviously thought people expected it of him. Even in a private gathering he felt honour-bound to put on a show. Of course we were all delighted, but I have to say that months later, when I heard of his collapse and death on stage in April 1984, it came as no surprise to me.

Making people laugh is a very exhausting business – ask any comedian – and I've never been able to work out how a man like Ken Dodd is able to entertain his audiences for up to five hours a night and then do it all over again the next night, and very often the night after that. 'Doddy' with his solo marathon mirth-making is exceptional, of course. Your average 'stand-up' on the thriving comedy circuit today would never choose to emulate the great man, and wisely so in my opinion. Like the miraculous Max Miller, there'll never be another Ken Dodd.

When one talks of comedians, Croydon rarely gets a distinguished mention and if you know my birthplace as I do, you'll agree that it's hardly a laugh-a-minute location. Don't tell the splendid Roy Hudd, though. He and I were born in the borough in the very same year (shall I tell 'em, Roy?). It was 1936, and our schooldays were spent there, it seems, sitting in the dark of the numerous cinemas that flourished just after the war.

We've compared notes over the years and I reckon he and I must have simultaneously thrilled to the (H) certificate 'horrors' of Karloff and Lugosi in the Scala and more exotic fare of the Palladium on Crown Hill. Roy and I also shared the delights of the music hall with our 'grown-ups' at the Croydon Empire in the high street, and both remember seeing Max Miller appear there on more than one occasion. Today, Roy is a man of many, many parts (all of them beautifully formed) and certainly fulfilled one of his life's ambitions when agreeing to play Archie Shuttleworth – the cheery undertaker –– in Coronation Street.

Variety is very much the spice of Huddy's life, and if you think I'm being over-familiar, then you've clearly not attended one of his wonderful pantomimes. On his very first, colourful appearance (usually in the 'Town Square') Roy beseeches the kids in the audience to bellow ''Allo 'Uddy !!' throughout the show the moment they catch sight of him. The response is immediate and deafening and what panto should be all about.

I envy Roy his role in promoting the theatre in this way, and for his tireless work on behalf of theatrical charities. Roy is also president of the Max Miller Appreciation Society of which (at the time of writing) I am chairman – so the two Croydon lads do get together occasionally. Michael Kilgarriff in his excellent book *Grace, Beauty and Banjos* – the peculiar lives and strange times of music hall and variety artistes through their billings – lists Roy as being 'the Peculiar Person' and describes him, quite rightly, as a National Treasure. I'd go along with that Michael, and would only add that it's been a pleasure knowing this 'treasure'.

But hey – that's quite enough name-dropping for the moment. It's time to return to that TWA flight from Los Angeles to London with young John Henty aboard and his new American friend, Phil. It's Wednesday, 6th July, 1960 and dawn is breaking over Heathrow Airport.

Ten-pin bowling is about to hit Croydon – but is Croydon ready for ten-pin bowling?

17

As Phil and I were soon to discover, within days of arriving in the UK, if we'd been carrying a quarter of a million pounds in our personal hand luggage, operation 'Ten-pin' would have been an unmitigated success. A top man with Croydon council pointed us in the direction of agents with town centre land to develop. Brunswick in London were eager to co-operate with the go-getting 'entrepreneurs' from the west coast, and I introduced Phil to several business contacts of mine, including a car dealership owner and a family friend who ran a successful laundry.

In other words, we made all the right moves with everyone agreeing that the idea was a good one, but it needed money up-front – and that was the one thing that we lacked big-time. Phil, of course, enjoyed himself enormously, never having been outside America before, and I was warmly welcomed home by everyone with the notable exception of Julie, who must have been ever-so-slightly miffed by my sudden re-appearance. Leaving dramatically 'for ever' is one thing. Returning with a madcap idea within months is entirely another.

In the end, the nearest I came to bringing an 'exciting new American leisure-time activity' to the burgeoning borough of Croydon was penning a feature article about the sport for the *Croydon Advertiser*. In it I explained why the town would enjoy ten-pin bowling and where I thought a centre should be established. Eventually, of course, one was opened but not where I envisaged and, it has to be said, like other centres across the UK, it never proved as popular here as it was in the States. Perhaps Phil and I had providence on our side? He went off to tour Europe before returning home to marry his beloved Caroline in California.

I returned to the *Advertiser* as a feature writer. Neither of us had any regrets about our barmy business venture and neither of us became bankrupt in the process. 'Put it down to experience' my father said re-assuringly – and predictably. It was certainly that.

Another experience was being sent to cover the activities of a council estate several miles from the centre of Croydon, at New Addington, within days of arriving back on the newspaper. Imagine it – one minute you're driving up Highway 101 linking Los Angeles with Santa Barbara in southern California; the next (well it seemed like the next) you're powering up Lodge Lane on your way to cover the monthly meeting of the

Addington Community Association. From the sublime to the ridiculous? Could be.

A few changes had been made in the reporter's room at 36, High Street, during the eight months I was away. Old time chief reporter Harold Snelling had been replaced by 'big-time' Geoff Bayliss, and there was a new woman on the block – a quite remarkable, avant-garde individual who later in life, went on to become one of this country's top feminist writers. Even as a humble 19-year old cub reporter, Angela Carter was way ahead of her time. She wore wild, ethnic gear from what I can remember. She liberally used four-

My photograph of the hugely talented Angela Carter and her first husband, Paul.

letter words to pep up her enthusiastic conversation (when this was practically unknown among male members of staff) and she had what I can only describe as a wicked, witch's cackle of a laugh. She smoked 'roll yer own' fags and she ate lots of yoghurt. Unbelievable.

Angela was great fun to be with and hugely talented too, although mundane court or council matters did not appeal and she never made any secret of this fact. Above all, she had the most vivid of imaginations, teetering on the surreal, and I am the proud owner of a paperback monthly magazine 'Storyteller' for July 1962 (price half-a-crown) which nominated Angela as 'our author of the month'.

Her prize-winning story was titled: 'The Man Who Loved A Double Bass' – 'her shape was that of a full-breasted, full-hipped woman, recalling certain primitive effigies of the Mother Goddess.' In the opening paragraph, we read: 'The consciously eccentric are always respectful and admiring of those who have the courage to be genuinely a little mad.' Angela had that courage in abundance, and we all enjoyed her eccentricity as well.

Young tea-throwing Joe Steeples and I spent many happy evenings round at Ms. Carter's flat in south Croydon which she shared with Paul, a record producer/musician, and when they removed to Bristol to enable Angela to get her degree in English we visited their new home in Clifton Place. Many years on, I saw a rather serious Angela appearing in a somewhat pretentious television programme as a panel member and was delighted to note that she'd not lost the 'cackle', which came bubbling through incongruously on a couple of occasions. 'That's 'our Ange', I thought to myself. In February 1992, Angela died of lung cancer at the age of 52.

New Addington was a challenge, I'll say that for it, and much of the page then devoted to the estate was taken up with court cases and news of discontented tenants complaining about everything from rising damp to rising bus fares into Croydon. Not that it was gloom and misery all of the time. I met some great characters there from Mrs. Dorothy Hook, auxiliary secretary of the RSPCA, – 'Don't sit on that chair, Mr. Henson, one of the cats has got the mange!' – to the delightfully-named Mrs. Codling who made the most delicious bread pudding for customers in the community centre. In fact it was so scrumptious that I even penned a poem in praise of the pud:

> *Mrs. Codling's Bread Pudding*
> *Had them coming from miles around.*
> *There were very few other good reasons*
> *For appearing NEW ADDINGTON bound!*
>
> *It was TALL, it was dark, it was handsome*
> *It was perfect for tea or for dinner*
> *It was cheap, quite unique, it was BRITISH,*
> *MRS. CODLING'S DISTINGUISHED BREAD-WINNER!*

My biggest problem in covering the district known to all in Croydon as Little Siberia was the fact that John Deadman, the Addington reporter for our rival newspaper, the *Croydon Times*, actually lived on the estate and obviously knew all the right people for a decent quote. Additionally, he was able to stay right to the end of a meeting while I would have chosen to opt out early in order to get back to my south Croydon home before midnight. You'd be surprised how many good stories emerged during 'Any Other Business'.

It used to drive me mad when, just as I was closing the notebook with a weary sigh of relief, some nasal-sounding guy would stand up and whine: 'On a point of order, Reg . . .' Under my breath I'd mutter 'Oh, no, not the issue of cars parked in Central Parade again – haven't you got a home to go to ?' John Deadman would smile and start taking more notes.

He had a home to go to and it was probably less than five minutes' walk from the centre.

I have to admit, the day I completed my final story in New Addington, I did speed along King Henry's Drive with all the windows of my Morris car rolled down, shouting at the top of my voice 'I'm free! I'm free!' It was Thursday, 26th October, 1961, and I was off to pastures new - well, Beckenham and Penge actually.

It was around this time too that I became involved with hospital broadcasting in the Croydon area. In my own newspaper I'd read of a man who was planning to start relaying football commentaries at Selhurst Park – the home of Crystal Palace FC – to several of the local hospitals, including Croydon General and Mayday. For a long term Palace supporter, and someone who aspired to be a broadcaster, this was surely too good an opportunity to miss. I immediately contacted organiser, Roy Preston. We met for a drink, and seven days later we were 'on air'.

It was 6th September, 1961 – a Wednesday evening under floodlights, pouring rain and our commentary position was in the back row of the main stand with no sound-proofing and every word we spoke over-heard by those around us. It was a strange arrangement. At the start we had no voice link with the participating hospitals and simply began broadcasting by plugging in a few gadgets under our reserved seats and talking into ancient lip microphones. Whether any of the patients could actually hear what we were saying was unclear, and whether they actually wanted to hear Palace losing 4–1 on a wet evening in south London, was equally questionable.

Conditions did improve though in the months and years ahead. We built our own customised studio (well, a garden shed actually) on the muddy terracing opposite the main stand the following season, and the team of three commentators established a cheery rapport and covered some pretty impressive cup and league games. I loved every moment of it, and my only problem was curbing my vociferous enthusiasm when the lads in claret and blue actually scored a goal while I was commentating. It was not that we were supposed to be unbiased as broadcasters (nobody bothered about that.). It was simply that a Palace goal was a rare event and I felt obliged to cheer my headphoned head off.

The solution, certainly in the garden shed days, was to announce the goal and moves leading up to it and then feed up the crowd reaction on our outside microphones while rushing to the door, opening it and screaming at length 'GOOOOAAAAL!' (And you thought Jonathan Pearce was excitable.) It was during the shed days that we were occasionally asked by the club to take over the public address responsibilities at first team home matches. Of the three of us, I was the one who most enjoyed this new role as it also meant introducing music, announcing team changes and seeing behind the scenes at Selhurst Park.

Before long the job was offered to me on a permanent basis, and I am sure you will believe me when I say that the 30 or so remarkable years that followed as 'Voice of the Palace' would warrant a book in their own right. For now though, suffice it to say, they were great times and perhaps my proudest achievement was to introduce the club's signature tune: 'Glad All Over' by the Dave Clark Five, which still echoes around SE25 when Palace are at home. I've even debated having it played at my funeral, but kindly friends have suggested that this idea might not be entirely appropriate.

The commentating though was an enormously valuable experience. Put it this way. If you can talk for 90 minutes non-stop (and there were occasions when I had to) and describe a 3–2 home defeat by mediocre Bristol City on a pre-Christmas Saturday afternoon, then – as Kipling might have put it (although he probably supported Brighton and Hove Albion) – 'You'll be a broadcasting man, my son'. Not only that, it provided me with an additional string to my journalistic bow and gave me the confidence to await that broadcasting break.

It was six years in coming.

18

Meantime, Beckenham beckoned. *The Beckenham and Penge Advertiser* had a district office in the high street which consisted of a front reception area ruled over by Ethel Twaites (really!), and a back room where the reporters typed their stories for a couple of days, drank copious cups of Ethel's tea and played the occasional game of Monopoly.

The chief reporter was yet another real character – a man who I shall always believe never quite fulfilled his true potential. Peter Jones lived in Brixton, went on exotic holidays alone, loved an argument and even wrote a raunchy first novel *The Leather Pluckers*, which was given a rave review by the BBC's Kenneth Allsop. To my knowledge it was Peter's only book. Somehow he seemed happier bashing out the minutiae of council minutes and devising droll comments on local affairs for a weekly notes column – a classic case, perhaps, of a biggish fish merrily splashing about in a small pond.

It was not how I saw things though. As with Angela, council meetings depressed me. Bromley magistrates court was a chore, and while for a time I enjoyed Ethel's banter through the hatch from the front office and the company of my fellow reporters, including Joe Steeples, my aim was to move on. On the final day of 1961 I wrote prophetically, in my diary: 'Of one thing I am quite certain. I will not be working for the *Advertiser* this time next year.'

So against a backdrop of tedious bus journeys, further unrequited passion and lots of sweet and sour pork (as more and more Chinese restaurants opened in the area), I started the search for pastimes and pastures anew. There was an interview, followed by a weird weekend in a builder's yard close by Heathrow Airport, for a radio presenter's job with – wait for it – The Voice of Slough. A Canadian entrepreneur, John Thompson, was determined to start a pirate radio station off the east coast with the call-sign: GBLN At The Nore.

I only got as far as the builder's yard where he had built a temporary (very temporary) studio complex. We got on well enough, but I sensed problems and made my excuses. There was a job with Westward Television in Plymouth, voice-over work for Voices Agency and a press officer position with British European Airways in Lower Regent Street, near Piccadilly Circus in London.

The airline's public relations department was looking for a feature-writing journalist who would be able to produce travel articles for syndication to provincial newspapers around the country. With my letter of application, I enclosed a cutting from the *Croydon Advertiser* of a feature I wrote following an inaugural flight from Gatwick Airport to Rotterdam by British United Airways (BUA).

Apparently, it was just the sort of thing Neville Haynes, the deputy chief public relations officer, was looking for, and at the subsequent interview in London he headed the panel that decided I was the right man for this plum job. Goodbye then to Ethel and her cups of tea and sympathy, to Peter and his eccentricities and to Sunday morning meetings of the Penge Trades Council in the unlikely setting of the Royston Ballroom.

The world was seemingly my oyster – or at least the European section of it – and while my main day-to-day responsibility was to answer press enquiries relating to BEA and its operations, I was also expected to produce regular travel features highlighting new destinations, aircraft and holiday promotions. This part of my job was soon to be nicknamed 'John Henty's Pie' by Neville Haynes's boss, the chief public relations officer, Bill Simpson.

Bill was an extraordinary man. Severely injured during aerial combat in the war, he had been one of plastic surgeon Archie McIndoe's 'Guinea Pigs' at East Grinstead and had had his face and both hands totally re-constructed. Bill had a wicked sense of humour which served him well and he also had an admirable knack of getting on with the airline's top brass. Crucially for the job, he was well respected by Fleet Street's aviation correspondents and travel writers. Happily, he appreciated my modest efforts and, more importantly, took the trouble to say so.

I started work at Dorland House in Lower Regent Street towards the end of August, 1962, and found myself sharing a third-floor room with two other press officers, Ken Cook and Dudley Foy. On my very first day I was whisked off to Heathrow Airport by Dudley to meet a glamorous American long-distance swimmer off a flight from Gibraltar.

At the airport we linked up with our man there, Harry Berry, who worked from a small office in Terminal One with his assistant, Molly Carter. This was the first of many celebrity encounters for me. In the next five years I assumed responsibility for, among others, The Beatles, Mary Ure's baby, the James Bond Film Unit and the entire Count Basie orchestra.

It was exciting stuff, as we shall discover, but Mary Margaret, the all-American swimmer, was enough to be getting on with on that first frenzied Monday, and after Dudley and I dropped her off in central London, I made for home in Croydon, suitably elated and in urgent need of a couple of aspirins.

I soon learned in my first week that Dudley Foy was, shall we say, the 'fixer' – the guy who'd go anywhere and do anything as long as it kept him out of the office. Ken, on the other hand, was the mainstay of the press office. You could rely totally on a quote from Mr. Cook, and if he didn't have the answer himself he always knew someone somewhere who did. Ken was meticulous, measured in his manner and, more importantly, a fellow Crystal Palace supporter. We all got on well together.

Producing the Henty features pie, as Bill called it, was my pigeon – a pigeon pie I suppose, and it didn't take me long to realise that if I was to write 750 words about the Costa Del Sol for example, it would be helpful to see the place first. In this respect, working for an airline that was beginning to operate regular flights to Malaga on Spain's southern coast, was a major advantage.

Using this logic in the months and years ahead, I was able to visit most of BEA's European destinations, and my first excursion was a there-and-back flight to Hamburg in the spring of 1963 when I was hosted by PR man Gerry Katzsch and his wife. Within days of my return from Germany, I was off again, this time heading for Malaga where I intended to explore the all-inclusive holiday market and growth of package holidays to places like Torremolinos.

And here I have a dreadful confession to make. In March of 1963, Torremolinos – where BEA had a small office under its superintendant, Arthur Frye – was a relatively quiet, relaxed and unspoiled fishing village. It had a central cafe on the main street where everybody hung out. The Quitapenas Bar produced the most devastating champagne cocktails and genuine flamenco dancing was to be seen nightly at the Bodega Andaluza.

I fell in love with the place and was completely knocked out by the energy and excitement generated by Emi Bonilla and his ravishing partner, Ana Maria. Nothing wrong in that, of course, but my enthusiasm for the 'village' and its surrounding countryside was soon put in writing (after all that was the purpose of my going there, wasn't it?) and subsequently syndicated to newspapers right across the UK. From Dundee to Dagenham, the cuttings came pouring in. They all liked the feature and their readers were planning to head for the Costa Del Sol in their thousands.

I have felt a tinge of guilt ever since, although obviously I was not alone in extolling the virtues of Andalusia – just one of the first to write about it. Gibraltar too came in for some Henty hype, but for totally different reasons. I flew down to the Rock on numerous occasions, including one bizarre trip in the company of hunky singer Eden Kane and a Page Three girl, Debbie. His hit single at the time – it went to No. 1 in the charts for a week – was 'Well I Ask You!', which summed up the promotional activity rather well. Eden found it difficult to perform with local musicians at the Rock Hotel one evening. Debbie refused to perform when approached by the manager of a well-known hotel across the water in Tangiers two days later.

I liked Gibraltar a lot. Yes, it was claustrophobic, noisy and often shrouded in a thick layer of cloud, but the people were friendly, the main street was fascinating and the pro-British feeling was all-pervasive. I made a number of good friends there over the years, including a lovely man, Pepe Brew, who had the Wimpy Bar concession on the Rock and was also a political commentator for the local TV station.

It was not unknown for Pepe to be serving a Wimpy burger and chips one moment and then, 20 minutes later, to be interviewing a senior union official about possible redundancies in the dockyards. Pepe and his family always made me more than welcome, and on one trip he and I completed a circular tour of Andalusia which took in Jerez de la Frontera, Toledo, Granada, Malaga and Marbella – all this at the height of the summer and without arranging any accommodation in advance.

One night, in the middle of nowhere, we booked into the Pension Jesus (which may have echoed my comment when I saw the bed on offer). The room fronted onto a very noisy town square. The shower was a tap high up on a wall with a piece of string attached, and breakfast was served in the owner's living room with a television on full blast. Around this time, the Spanish leader, Franco, was seeking re-election, with the proud boast: '25 Years of Peace'. Not in this town, I thought to myself. It was a fascinating journey though, and certainly made yet another packaged 'pie' for the UK provincial press.

This year, 1963, was exciting all-round, and in April I found myself on what can only be described as a dream assignment. Eon Film Productions were about to film their second James Bond movie 'From Russia With Love' and I was about to travel to Istanbul with 007 himself, Sean Connery. Not only Mr. Connery though. The entire production unit, led by Harry Salzman and 'Cubby' Broccoli, were aboard the BEA Vanguard on a murky Saturday morning towards the end of April – quite a responsibility for the aircrew when one thinks about it, and a fair amount of PRessure for

John Henty. I was joined by sales representative, Wally Walton, whose BEA brief in London was to service the needs of the entertainments industry. It was thanks to Wally that Eon had chosen the Vanguard to transport them to Turkey. In a highly competitive business, Wally pointed out that the turbo-prop aircraft was a fine workhorse and more than capable of carrying tons of film equipment as well as the actual film crew.

And what a mixed bunch we had aboard! In addition to Bond, there was the obligatory blonde (an actress called Daniela Bianchi) for whom this movie was the 'big break'. She sat apart for much of the flight, and I got a gorgeous photograph of her – completely relaxed – which was used in the BEA magazine to accompany my article. Co-starring with Connery was the fine Shakespearean actor Robert Shaw, and he spent much of the four-hour flight via Rome playing cards with the stuntmen who were seated together at the rear.

I particularly like this photograph I took of actress Daniela Bianchi aboard a BEA Vanguard aircraft bound for Istanbul and location filming for the second James Bond movie 'From Russia with Love' – April 1963.

The Mexican actor Pedro Armendariz kept up a continuous banter with all and sundry in the gangway, and I heard him enthusiastically discussing the finer points (if there are any) of belly dancing with Eon's publicity man. It was only two months later that I read of the actor's death in a Los Angeles hospital at the age of 51. On his return to the west coast from filming Bond, he had been diagnosed with cancer of the spine and given one year to live. Allegedly, a gun was smuggled into his hospital and he shot himself.

I can remember that the news of his death, and the nature of it, depressed me enormously on a Wednesday in June. I'd welcomed him and his co-stars back to the UK on 16th May, and on that occasion I had an even more bizarre role to perform on behalf of Robert Shaw. While away filming in Turkey, his (how shall I put this?) amour, the actress Mary Ure, had given birth to their child and flown to Istanbul with the baby to be with him on location.

They returned together aboard the chartered Vanguard, and the airport press had obviously got wind of this. They all wanted a photograph of the couple with their new baby. The couple, needless to say, wanted no part in this and told me so when I boarded the aircraft on the tarmac. I was firmly impaled on the horns of a dilemma. Passengers aboard our aircraft were my responsibility, wearing a public relations hat – especially if they were newsworthy passengers – but, on the other hand, donning my press officer's pork pie, I had to look after the needs of the press at Heathrow on a day-to-day basis.

What to do? Well, on this occasion, I sided with the VIP passengers and agreed to smuggle Ms Ure's new baby through a little-used exit gate while mum and dad, backed by their colleagues, protested their innocence. 'Baby, what baby? There is no baby!' In fact, there *was* a baby and fortunately it slept soundly for the 20 minutes that I crept through Customs, tiptoed through Arrivals and waited anxiously by the Terminal Two taxi-rank.

Heavens knows what would have happened if the very young child had awoken and started crying. Explain that away to the airport police. I had enough difficulty putting my side of the story across to a very irate *Daily Sketch* photographer later.

'What was I to do, Reg? I mean – they left me holding the baby, didn't they?'

Reg was not impressed and probably never forgave me, but I had another job to do on that Thursday afternoon in May and that involved welcoming home the Tottenham Hotspur football team who had just won the European Cup Winners Cup in Rotterdam the night before. They came off their BEA Comet aircraft carrying the cup aloft, but who was it do you think who actually staggered through Customs with it

Right first time! That was quite a day. I'd won a cup and had a baby – all in the space of three hours.

19

I was soon to discover that not all press officer work involved film units off to exotic locations and accompanying press parties on inaugural flights all over Europe. Much of our time was spent answering the most basic of enquiries about industrial relations, airline food and the annual report and accounts.

I remember one BEA story that ran and ran in newspapers and radio stations right across the world and that was the case of the exploding

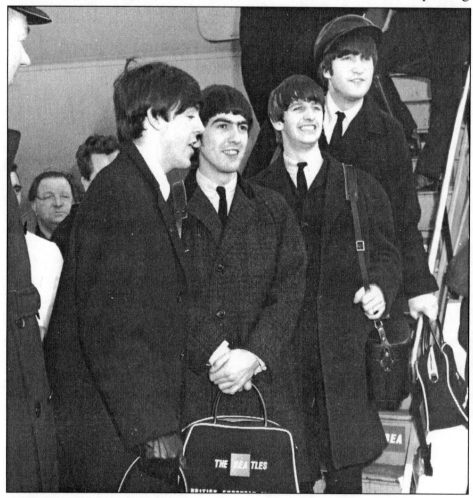

I came up with the BEAtles flight bag idea after escorting the Fab Four through Heathrow Airport in October 1963. [BEA photo]

marshmallow. Please don't ask! All I can remember is that under certain cabin air pressures a free sweet offered to BEA passengers about to land was 'popping' off the plate in a white cloud of powdered sugar . . . allegedly. A daft Sixties story, probably created during Fleet Street's annual 'silly season' during the summer, but publicity for the airline nevertheless and a laugh for world-wide readers. Our cuttings service was inundated for weeks with material relating to the combustible confection.

Late one Tuesday evening in October, just as I was about to leave the Dorland House office for home, the duty phone rang and, with a degree of reluctance, I answered – to find myself talking to the Beatles' manager, Brian Epstein, in Liverpool. He sounded under pressure and was concerned about the arrangements for the 'boys' on their flight to Stockholm the next day aboard a BEA Comet.

This was before the mass hysteria stuff, but with 'She Loves You' topping the charts and sell-out concert appearances completed across the UK, the 28-year-old Brian was anxious to ensure the safe departure of his valuable foursome. I did my best to re-assure him and promised that I would personally meet the group in departures the next morning. I knew Harry at the airport was away, with his assistants Molly and Linda covering for him, so before I left the office I rang them at Heathrow with an early-morning warning: BEWARE BEATLES!

The next morning (early), having driven across from Croydon on relatively quiet roads, I parked the car and made my way to European Departures. There I soon picked out the unmistakable figures of John, Paul, George and Ringo – not a difficult task because I had seen them in concert at the Fairfield Halls in Croydon a few weeks before and, inevitably on this sunny Wednesday morning, they were creating quite a stir amongst their fellow passengers.

Strangely, though, they appeared to be unaccompanied – wandering freely about the concourse, buying newspapers and chatting among themselves. There was certainly no sign of Epstein, and not a hint of 'minders' or security staff. Imagine! This is where I stepped in, bringing them together and pointing out that we would drive to the aircraft in a BEA vehicle. Forget the concept of a stretched limousine – once through passport control we all piled into a small airside van with Lennon sitting next to the driver ('Wait till I tell the grandchildren!') and John Henty, Paul, George and Ringo squashed in at the rear.

From what I can recall, each of the lads was carrying his own stage suit on a hanger, over his arm, with no sign of a guitar. The conversation was frenetic and daft. The journey out to the waiting Comet took only two to three minutes. Despite the early hour, the airport press had assembled and the photographers were soon busy – shouting their instructions and getting the Liverpool lads to leap about and generally behave as they felt a pop group should.

At this point I was a mere supernumerary but I managed to take a few photographs of my own to complement the work of BEA's own staff photographer. It struck me at the time that it would have been better for the airline if our distinctive red square logo had been more in evidence during this zany photo-session. Weeks later, when I learned that the group was returning from yet another European gig – this time in Paris – I came up with an idea which I phoned over to Harry at the airport. 'Why don't we provide them with BEA hand luggage bearing our logo but with the added letters 'THE BEATLES' permanently affixed?' Harry liked the idea a lot and immediately made contact with the suppliers, who produced the goods in double-quick time.

Gimmicky ideas are always a gamble – we recognised this – but happily the Beatles played along with our plan and carried the distinctive bags on more than just the one overseas trip. In fact they may very well have taken one or two across to the USA when things began to hot up for them over there. I do know today that a similar bag came up for auction in London recently and fetched a figure well in excess of a thousand pounds. And no, I don't have any spare examples in my loft – just memories and a few photographs of that October morning in 1963.

In fact 1963 was turning out to be quite a year. Apart from James Bond in April and the Beatles in October, I also covered the Isle of Man TT races in June when a BEA Sikorsky helicopter was employed to provide a rapid response unit. I flew to the island of Crete in September with another film unit on location. This time it was a Walt Disney movie, 'The Moonspinners', starring Hayley Mills and some owl extras, overseen by Mary Chipperfield, who all crammed aboard the ever-reliable Vanguard aircraft. What a hoot! Mind you, they could have flown El Owl I suppose, but Wally Walton had obviously been at work once again.

In August I was crop-spraying north of Edinburgh. In November, the British Guild of Travel Writers held their annual general meeting in Malta and their flight arrangements and itinerary on the island became my responsibility. I struck up a friendship with several of the country's leading travel correspondents on this five-day trip and over the years, developed these contacts from that of business to a more personal relationship. John Carter, for example, was travel editor for the Thomson group of newspapers about this time and had brought his wife Sheila and one of his daughters to Malta. We hit it off immediately, and John and Sheila were both at my wedding the following year. Veteran broadcaster Wynford Vaughan Thomas was the life and soul of the party at the Phoenicia Hotel in Valetta, and I also got to know another distinguished writer, bearded S.J. Rossiter-Shepherd (or Ross Shepherd), who was the *People* newspaper's top travel man. Ross was a most flamboyant character who loved his food and wine and was pretty adept when it came to flamenco dancing: he even carried his own castanets around with him in case of an emergency.

It was my first visit to . . . [EDITOR: *Just a minute, please, could we go over that last paragraph with reference to the charming John Carter fellow. The one who eventually went on to greater things with the 'Holiday' programme which he devised for the BBC and then 'Wish You Were Here' on ITV. Did you say, Mr. Henty – John . . . Did you say that Carter and his wife attended your . . . wedding in 1964? You did? Fine! Perhaps you could go into a little more detail about that. I mean, you've built up this pathetic image of being the innocent victim of unrequited love. Not quite what I heard from a certain Christina, John! And then, suddenly, it's requited – hearts and flowers – homes and gardens – love and marriage. Bit more detail, John boy . . . and when I say detail, I mean detail. Know what I mean? Know what I . . .*]

As I was saying, it was my first visit to Malta and, rather like Gibraltar, I enjoyed the pro-British feeling there then and the friendliness of the island's indigenous inhabitants. I vowed to return and did so in the spring of 1965 when I was able to take my wife, Sylvia [EDITOR: *About time!*] with me on what we both regarded as our second honeymoon.

I met Sylvia the day after I had been told of actor Pedro Armendariz's death in Hollywood. The news had depressed me to the point where I wrote in my diary on Thursday, 20th June, 1963, of 'a very great tragedy', and added bleakly: 'Life? Ugh!'

That evening, at a very loose end indeed, I got out my newly acquired Volkswagen Beetle and drove away from my parents' home in south Croydon with no particular destination in mind. I could have made for Land's End in Cornwall or South End in Croydon. As it was I ended up at a local park where I knew a branch of the Young Conservatives were intent on playing a game of rounders. Now that is desperate! To be fair, though, in those days, the YCs were a flourishing organisation nationwide with a raunchy reputation for good social events and very little politics. That suited me fine, and it seems that Sylvia, who was living in nearby Beddington, held the same view. She travelled over to south Croydon on a whim that Thursday evening – made a change from a bus she told me later – when she could so easily have stayed in and watched the television or played some records.

We were both outsiders and played the game without noticing each other, and it was only as the event came to a close that our paths, so to speak, crossed. Sylvia joined two other girls in accepting a lift home in the bright red VW. The fact that she was last to be dropped off was purely geographical but for me it was happily providential too. I enjoyed our brief parting conversation and asked whether she was planning to participate in a car rally to the west Sussex coast at the weekend. Sylvia was non-committal, but as I drove away, I thought to myself 'I do hope she'll turn up' – and, two days later, she did. I was delighted and according to the diary on the Sunday, 'spent a relaxed time on the beach in pleasant company'.

Sylvia Mary Allen was 21 years of age when we met and was living with her parents and two younger brothers in a pleasant neighbourhood on the outskirts of Croydon. The one abiding memory I have of her home was the strong smell of chocolate from time to time, largely in the rear garden, which was caused by the close proximity of George Payne's chocolate factory – he of the yummy Poppets. That sort of pollution I could live with.

At the time, Sylvia's parents ran a sub-post office and wool shop in Beckenham. Her brothers were at local schools and she was working on nearby Purley Way for the well-known Lambretta scooter company. Sylvia was born in Kettering, Northamptonshire, during the war but moved with her parents to south London after the war and was educated at a school in South Norwood.

This wasn't just any part of London SE25, though. The Lady Edridge Grammar School for Girls was next door to the home of Crystal Palace Football Club, and from their classroom windows the girls were able to watch young professional footballers go through their paces in preparation for match days.

In this slightly unusual way, Sylvia became interested in the fortunes of the Palace and occasionally attended first team games with her youngest brother, John, who she used to lift over the turnstiles to enter one of the wing stands at Selhurst Park. A mutual interest in what was then, in 1963,

The Beatles again – and a barrage of jelly babies

Third Division football may seem an odd factor now in bringing two people closer together, but it certainly helped for Sylvia and me, and over the years our joint enthusiasm has never diminished.

It's wobbled a bit for me, I have to admit, but together we've enjoyed the highs and lows of English football. We made Wembley for a couple of finals. I operated the public address system during three promotion seasons to the First Division 68/69, 78/79 and 88/89. We were at Villa Park when Palace defeated Liverpool by four goals to three during extra time in the 1990 FA Cup semi-final.

Cynics will probably suggest that Miss Allen only agreed to go out with me because of my Palace connections and cheap flight concessions with BEA, They would be wrong. We enjoyed each other's company right from the start. My mum and dad thought the world of her, and so did I. The fact that Sylvia also liked eating out, travelling and watching any football on the box was a bonus. We were 'going steady' and things were looking up for me as I approached my 28th birthday.

We both remember seeing the Beatles in Croydon on Saturday, 7th September, 1963. I still kept in touch with former colleagues on the *Croydon Advertiser*, and as a result I was offered two press tickets for 'The Beatles Show'. Apparently, no one else was interested in a job on a Saturday evening.

The remarkable thing about the two-show Mersey package was that the foursome were only one of five groups to appear that night, and the event even had a compere. Comedian Ted King never stood a chance, of course. The screaming audience tolerated Ian Crawford and The Boomerangs. Mike Berry and The Innocents just about survived, but Rockin' Henri and the Hayseeds? Well, they were howled off the stage, and a local band (who all went to my former school, by the way) Patrick Dane's Quiet Five had about five minutes to make themselves heard. Quiet it was not. Then a terrified-by-now Ted King announced 'T H E   B E A T L E S!' and probably ran for it – never to be seen again. Total pandemonium, and I have never witnessed scenes like it since. Sylvia and I were sitting about 12 rows from the front. We heard not a single word of any song and we were pelted throughout by boxes of jelly babies and loose jelly babies. I think it may have been George Harrison who had foolishly expressed a liking for . . . jelly babies.

I certainly expressed a liking for the Beatles in my subsequent review. I wrote: 'They were self-assured, smart in appearance and gave the customers what they wanted – although what that precisely was is a good question.' I went on: 'During their 15-minute appearance on stage the numbers they played included, I believe . . . ' (Some guesswork on my part for I'd not heard a word, and it was all over, as I commented, in 15 frenzied minutes.

Not so long ago, older but not necessarily wiser, Sylvia and I attended a pre-Christmas performance by the 'Bootleg Beatles' in Brighton. They looked fine. They fooled around convincingly. They sang the songs. But the trouble was – we could hear every word and . . . there were no jelly babies.

20

B ack in 1963 the genuine Beatles continued to make the headlines and BEA was able to grab some of the associated glory. The airline provided a helicopter for the crazy dance sequence filmed from the air by producer Richard Lester at Gatwick Airport. The movie? 'A Hard Day's Night'. I got involved with the Beatles Christmas show at the Finsbury Park Astoria in north London and attended what was meant to be a rehearsal on Christmas Eve. I described it as 'fun and games' in my diary, with the fab foursome ever-so-slightly out of control and continually larking about in the darkened auditorium.

By this time too, of course, their fame was spreading worldwide, and after two appearances on the legendary Ed Sullivan Show in the States – February 1964 – every American kid was chanting 'She Loves You' and there was even a look-alike group called the Bedbugs who I saw at the Paramount cinema in New York towards the end of March.

Interest was phenomenal, as I was to discover when I returned to the West Coast at the beginning of March. My boss, Bill Simpson, had agreed my visit ostensibly to observe the approach of our BOAC public relations colleagues in America. Clearly, I wanted to revisit friends in Santa Barbara four years on, and I also hoped to meet up with the legendary Mel Blanc in Hollywood. All this had to be achieved in 12 frantic days.

With me I carried the colour photographs which I took at Heathrow Airport when the Beatles departed for Stockholm in October 1963. When I produced these, together with the official BEA black and white photographs, out of a stiff brown envelope, in the offices of the Title Insurance and Trust Company in Santa Barbara, everything ground to a halt. I was immediately besieged by secretaries, senior staff and the guy who took over my job when I departed four years previously. They all wanted to see the Liverpool lads for themselves, and I was questioned about every aspect of my tenuous ties with the 'Crazy Brits.' Soon a management figure emerged to investigate what the disruption was all about, and I was asked – ever so diplomatically – to 'beetle' off back to 'Jolly Ol' England'. Yeah! Yeah! Yeah!

Before I did, though, I moved from Beatles to Bugs – Bugs Bunny and that interview in Hollywood. I arrived in Los Angeles aboard a Greyhound bus from Santa Barbara on Thursday, 12th March, 1964. There I made for the downtown BOAC offices where PR man David Lobb, told me – almost casually in our opening conversation – that the next day they were interviewing candidates for a position as BOAC press officer for the entire west coast of America and including Hawaii. Was I interested in applying? I was indeed, and found it very difficult to sleep that night in my overnight LA hotel.

The interview the following day – Friday the 13th, by the way – went well enough and I was able to impress David with my knowledge of the West Coast and broadcasting experience in Santa Barbara. I recognised, however, that the odds were heavily stacked against me and flew back to the UK a few days later without giving much further thought to what could turn out to be an enormous challenge. A challenge, that is, if I were given the job, and in all honesty I have never been a 'What if?' type of person. . . and anyway, BOAC were bound to call a second interview and that would be an even tougher test.

They did – and it was. Much to my amazement, seven days later, a cable was delivered to my desk at Dorland House which read: 'John Henty from Carter. Grateful you be in New York first thing Monday, March 30, for appearance – selection board'. The following day, 25th March, 1964, was my 28th birthday, and Sylvia and I talked things over at length while enjoying a Chinese meal. If I did get the job, we agreed, then life together on the West Coast of America would be rather exciting, and certainly an improvement on suburban south London.

The very real prospect of such a challenge certainly got us thinking about living together, and even though I was not chosen by BOAC two weeks later, far more importantly, I was 'chosen' by Sylvia to be her husband and we got engaged after selecting a ring in London's Hatton Garden. All together . . . aaaaaah!

The job interview was held in BOAC's New York office on Easter Monday and was organised along American lines. I was one of three candidates, and after individual interviews with the board we were all brought together and encouraged to talk through the introduction of a 'new aircraft' onto American routes, whilst the panel listened in.

This struck me as being slightly unreal and, as a result I suspect, my contributions were forced and a touch theatrical. In essence, I was role playing and, in the process, not being myself. I also had a lousy head-cold. Add to all this the fact that the other two guys hailed from the West Coast and were more familiar with the sort of thing expected of them at a board and you have a no-win situation for the man in the Union Jack suit.

BOAC summed it up thus: 'Our difficult decision in choosing the candidate for this job from amongst those who applied was ultimately decided in favor of an applicant whose existing contacts on the West Coast are quite extensive.'

I had no problem with that. The weekend in New York had been exciting, with the bonus of a live rock 'n' roll show starring Jackie Wilson and Lesley Gore. The interview experience had been enormously valuable and, after all, I had been on a very short list for a much sought after, prestigious job.

Privately, Sylvia and I were both relieved when the letter arrived from New York. Now we could get on with planning our life together in the UK, and the first step was – to buy that ring.

21

They say
Spike Milligan is
Ill agin
He's taken to his bed.
A mild dose
Of bellicose
Or humans in the head!

Everybody has written about Spike (that's my version above), and this is largely because everybody reckons they knew the man in one form or another. In truth, no-one really ever got to know him properly, and that included wives, 'sweethearts', children, fellow comedians, royalty and, to a large extent, the man himself.

I mention him now not because, chronologically, he played a part in my life during the 1960s but simply because, as an influence on most of my 'adult' life, he was always there – and occasionally our paths did cross. Like most people of my generation, I admired his anarchic approach to life and never missed a Goon Show on the radio if I could help it.

On a miserable October Sunday in 1957, I took a girl-friend, Kathy, to the Camden Theatre in north London to witness the recording of not one but *two* Goon Shows in one evening. The first was for Home Service consumption and the other was for the BBC World Service. Both were riotously funny and the comedy was aided and abetted, I suspect, by regular cries of 'Round the back for the old brandy!'

Spike was everywhere that evening and made frequent forays into the orchestra – much to the amusement of Peter Sellers and the giggly Harry Secombe. Max Geldray and the Ray Ellington Quartet provided the music and the audience just lapped it all up. How lucky we were to have seen the show when we did and no wonder, years later, that Peter Sellers spoke of those Sunday evenings as being 'The happiest times in a much-troubled life'.

Occasionally I would write to Spike with invitations to various innocuous events in the Croydon area and I was never really disappointed when there was no reply from the man or his faithful PA, Norma Farnes. Once though he did advertise in a national newspaper (probably the *Guardian*) for someone to cut his lawn when he was away in Australia, visiting his mother. This was too good an opportunity to miss and I submitted an urgent application which spoke of my 'growing mowing prowess' and recent work for HM the Queen Mother. All lies! Additionally, I enclosed a small, sealed plastic bag which contained grass from our own lawn and the note: 'You may be interested in some of my recent cuttings.' !

Needless to say, he wasn't interested and may not even have seen the package before departing Down Under. I'm sure Norma will have dealt with it appropriately and cursed the name John Henty in so doing. Perhaps that is why Spike always treated me (and others like me) with a fair degree of caution. Approachable he was not, and the two brief interviews I did achieve – one for the BBC and the other for hospital radio – were both stilted and awkward affairs. Spike would also suggest that he expected payment, and although this was done in a jocular fashion it created one or two difficult moments.

On the last occasion we met, I was invited to his house outside the East Sussex town of Rye, to record a selection of war poems on behalf of a freelance producer who knew Spike and accompanied me. On the wall, by the front door, I noticed a plaque which suggested that the sizeable detached property had been designed by a 'blind architect'. Only Milligan would have created such a sign, but I must say that I could not really understand why he had chosen to live there in the first place. It seemed a rather remote location to me, and the view from the main lounge was, shall we say, distinctly uninspiring.

On that afternoon, however, Spike was welcoming enough and clearly enjoyed talking about his shared war experiences and the colleagues he was still in touch with. At the end of the recording session though I quietly asked him whether he would mind signing a black and white photograph I had in my possession which showed him peering into a What The Butler Saw machine at the Towner Art Gallery in Eastbourne. The machine was mine, incidentally, and the photograph had been published in the *Eastbourne Gazette*.

Oh, dear! He did mind, and asked me why I wanted his autograph. He simply could not understand – on that particular afternoon at least – why I should want it. The nonchalant atmosphere in the lounge changed abruptly – a signature was not forthcoming and we left soon afterwards. My producer friend was not entirely amused.

Yet the antithesis of this sorry story is that years earlier, when I'd sent Spike a cassette recording of my radio programme praising his touring one-man show, he replied with a beautifully-signed copy of one of his early books of verse for children, now a prized possession.

That was the Spike I choose to remember along with the memory of a brilliant evening of stand-up comedy which he performed on Brighton's Palace Pier in October 1984 – in aid of the other pier. I compered that evening for the BBC and relish to this day his story of the jam roll which had reached its sell-by date.

Spike reached his sell-by date in February 2002, and I was privileged to attend the memorial service to him in London in June of that year. We all knew on that sunny Monday morning that no-one would ever replace Spike Milligan. As one newspaper predictably put it the following day: 'GOON BUT NOT FORGOTTEN'.

22

Spike, of course, was one of numerous celebrities who flew with British European Airways in the Sixties, and many of them started or ended their journeys at West London Air Terminal in Cromwell Road, SW7. I can remember the Rolling Stones stopping the traffic on one occasion. The Walker Brothers ever-so-slightly under the . . . weather, and even Sid James turning up in his TV role as a London cab driver. Then there was Tony Hancock (quite a handful).

Bill Simpson's public relations department moved to 'WLAT' from Lower Regent Street soon after Sylvia and I met, and this meant that when it came to finding our first home together we concentrated on London's west side, leading on to the M4 motorway. The Earls Court area was a happy hunting ground, and Sylvia would often join me after work for a meal in our favourite restaurant, which we still talk about today.

The first Stockpot was a mere boomerang's throw from the underground station in Brompton Road. It always had a queue outside and served the most delicious food at very reasonable prices. Our favourite meal was probably egg mayonnaise followed by chicken à la king with Dutch apple and cream or icecream and chocolate sauce – all for well under 7s 6d. No wonder the place was busy: a glass of water would arrive unasked, and all main meals came with chips and veg. of the day. The staff were friendly and efficient. The Stockpot name lives on in central London today and still gives value for money but the original was very special and we were regular customers in the mid-Sixties.

My public relations colleague Ken Cook had married a delightful Danish girl, Kirsten, and they had moved into a block of flats in west Kensington, close to the famous Queens Club. There was no way Sylvia and I were going to be able to afford a house in London – my salary just about topped a thousand pounds a year and she was earning considerably less as a secretary.

Rented accommodation was clearly the only feasible answer and, encouraged by the Cooks, we approached their estate office and established that £350 a year would buy us a lease on a sizeable apartment in Queens Club Gardens with our own porter and – not surprisingly perhaps – a tennis court in private grounds. Imagine what that would cost today!

But then again, take a brief look at my 'little red book' with the words 'Flat budget' written on it. My father, the accountant remember, drummed it into me on numerous occasions that I should keep a record of all personal finances, and when wedding bells began to ring he became even more emphatic: 'You must work out a budget for each room of your future home' he intoned, 'And keep within that budget or else . . .'

So Sylvia and I duly purchased a couple of those mini red cash books beloved of Woolworths, plus a red pen, and when agreement was reached with the Queens Club Gardens estate office on a second floor property in Milton Mansions (complete with Bob, the porter) we conscientiously wrote on the first page: 'Estimated expenditure': kitchen £80, bedroom £90, dining room £80, living room £50 and fittings £85 – total of £385 to fit and furnish the entire flat, which fortunately came with its own carpets but not curtains.

A down-payment on a gas cooker then was £4 7s 4d. Monthly re-payments for an electric fire were £1 7s 6d. My take-home pay from BEA for the month of November 1964 (just one month after getting married) was a mere £79 9s 5d, and it's true to say that we in the press office were unhappy with this and I was not the only member of Bill's talented team to start scanning the pages of *WPN* (*World's Press News*) for more remunerative employment.

Subsidised air travel was all very well, and I enjoyed the wide variety of work involved (especially my feature-writing 'pie'), but we knew we were not well paid, and marriage meant finding the monthly rent and trying to put something aside for the future – not at all easy when your joint income, with both partners working in London remember, was well under 50 quid a week.

We married on a Sunday in October and the vicar of Sylvia's local Congregational church in Beckenham had to seek special dispensation to allow us to hold the ceremony after his normal Sunday morning service. The reason for this unusual move was to enable Sylvia's parents to attend, which – as business people – they would not have been able to do on a normal weekday or Saturday afternoon.

Sylvia's many relatives travelled down from the Kettering area with the delightful Aunt Ena baking the cake and elderly grandfather getting his first taste of . . . Chinese food. We held our reception in a Chinese restaurant because it was the only one open on a Sunday afternoon in Beckenham High Street and, more importantly, we all liked Chinese food. Everyone received complimentary chopsticks. Ena's cake created a problem when it came to the cutting ceremony. The restaurant staff were not familiar with this time-honoured tradition and had great difficulty producing a suitable cutting implement. Our final memory – before being whisked away to Heathrow for a flight to Dublin – was of Sylvia's father being accosted outside the restaurant by an anxious waiter, clutching a large bill on a small plate. This was clearly their first wedding reception and probably their last, too. We enjoyed it.

The honeymoon was fine, and it certainly had its moments. We shared our first night together in Jury's Hotel, Dublin, with a drunken rugby team storming the corridors outside our room. In Cork, we were offered sweet and sour pork doused in tomato ketchup. In Killarney the sherry trifle was 80 per cent sherry and 20 per cent trifle. At Bunratty Castle we dined with Americans and, appropriately enough, toasted our future life together with glasses of mead. Certainly the Irish could not have been more welcoming and somehow they seemed to sense that we were 'newly-weds' and offered VIP treatment wherever our hired VW Beetle took us.

It was good, nevertheless, to return to our new west London apartment, and amusing to re-call now that the one item we had failed to purchase prior to the Big Day was a tin opener. After so much hotel food, we both fancied something simple like spaghetti on toast. The tin was produced. The toast was toasting. 'Where's the tin opener?' came the cry. 'What tin opener?' came the response. Hysterical collapse of both starving parties.

The early days in Queens Club Gardens were definitely fun. I was working now full-time at West London Air Terminal. Sylvia was temping in the West End through one or two secretarial agencies. We would eat out a lot (despite acquiring a tin opener) and enjoyed the London parks and going to the cinema, mostly at the Odeon in Kensington High Street – walking distance away.

At BEA the Henty features 'pie' continued to satisfy the demands of Bill Simpson and the UK provincial press, and there were inaugural parties of journalists and travel agents to host both in this country and in Europe. Gibraltar remained my favourite destination and I was hopping up and down to the Rock in the way that one might commute from London to Brighton. Sylvia was able to join me on occasions.

The broadcasting bug had never gone away though, and I continued to provide the public address entertainment for Crystal Palace. This meant making suitable announcements and spinning discs before the game for an hour or so and at half time. I enjoyed the work and, more importantly, the fans seemed to like my humorous approach behind the microphone.

One incident when I was Duty Press Officer at the Air Terminal on a Bank Holiday Monday though brought home to me the excitement of live radio. I was responsible for a BBC radio unit who were conducting interviews with the travelling public and then playing their choice of recorded music back in, presumably, Broadcasting House. The interviewer, I remember, was a woman and I couldn't help thinking to myself, as I hovered in the background, how that could be me – chatting to people, linking with the studio and broadcasting to the nation. I was impressed by this simple exercise, and even more so when I moved some distance away and listened to the end product on my new transistor radio (purchased in Main Street, Gibraltar).

Yes, I could do that – but again the question was how to get a job with the BBC. Unbeknown to me, the answer would be forthcoming within a year of that holiday request show. Local radio was under consideration for the UK, and the BBC had plans to open at least eight experimental radio stations including one on the south coast at Brighton. An impossible task, but be patient, John Henty . . .

23

WARNING! For those with delicate stomachs: skip the next two paragraphs

You know, I honestly believe that if I had whistled, the side salad of lettuce leaves, onion and tomato would have slowly slithered across the plastic table cloth towards me, and as for the calves brain omlette which accompanied it . . . well! Sylvia and I were aboard a Yugoslavian cruise boat anchored at Port Said in Egypt. October 1966, and I was to write about the experience for a Canadian newspaper.

I cannot quite remember how this came about. All I can recall is that we boarded the boat in Venice and were in the company of some rather eccentric people including the odd right honourable or two and a crew-cut executive from a major American corporation based in New York. They tucked into the food with gay abandon but Sylvia and I had seen the provisions being loaded aboard at Port Said and decided that a few slices of dry toast would be a safer proposition. It was a wise move on our part, and even more so for Sylvia who was not really enjoying the dubious diet and rushed itinerary.

In fact, after ship-hopping down the Dalmatian coast and dropping in on Malta momentarily, Sylvia and I decided that we would 'abandon' ship on arrival in Athens. She was feeling decidedly unwell and I knew that a daily BEA Athens/London Comet aircraft would soon whisk us home to the comfort of our flat and the re-assurance of something civilised on toast. The ship's fare had been dodgy in the extreme and anyway, dear Sylvia was about to discover that she also had a 'condition' to contend with. She was pregnant – and we were delighted.

Andrew John Henty was born seven months later on 27th May, 1967, in the Princess Beatrice hospital in the London borough of Chelsea and, no, I was not present at the actual birth. At that time, fathers were allowed to stay with their wives in the delivery room but this was not exactly encouraged by the hospital and, typically, Sylvia decided that she'd rather go-it-alone so to speak. I had no argument with this – knowing the sort of girl that I'd married and fully respecting her strong independent nature. The last thing Sylvia Allen wanted was an anxious John Henty mooching about in the background and making sympathetic noises. Well, that's how I saw it anyway.

Baby Andrew arrived in a thunderstorm at 6.35 pm and I arrived less than an hour later to share a cup of tea with Sylvia and hold our son for the first time as she looked on. He was remarkably peaceful – alongside rows of other yelling infants at the hospital – but we both realised, on returning to Queens Club Gardens, that a second-floor flat in west Kensington was no place for a new baby.

This was surely the moment to buy our first home, and we immediately started a trawl through estate agents' details. At the same time, I intensified my search for a better-paid job. Needless to say, everything came together at once. It always seems to, doesn't it ? We found and moved into an end-of-terrace property in Raynes Park. I read that the BBC was about to advertise for staff to open experimental local radio stations at places like Liverpool, Sheffield, Leicester, Stoke and Brighton. The stations would be on air within months, and interviews were planned for July. This was it! I immediately wrote-off to the BBC for an application form.

Of course I was not the only person living in hope, for this was truly seen as the big breakthrough in British broadcasting and everyone wanted a slice of the action – particularly those who were already members of BBC staff. Every technical operator from Lands End to John O' Groats, every Broadcasting House studio manager, every World Service supernumerary – they all recognised that local radio was a breath of fresh airwaves and wanted to be in at the start.

This, of course, was bad news for someone with similar aspirations but none of their breadth of live broadcasting experience. To say that the odds

When did you first see your father? Andrew is not convinced.

were heavily stacked against me would be a wild understatement but, undaunted, I made for the first interview in a building tantalisingly close to Broadcasting House.

I cannot remember whether I had stated on the form a preference for one specific radio station, but if I had done it would most certainly have been BBC Radio Brighton. It was fortunate, then, that the person conducting my initial interview was the manager designate for Brighton, Bob Gunnell, a man with an impressive BBC pedigree who lived in the town – well, Hove actually – and was already involved in local politics.

Until quite recently Bob had been producer of a popular magazine-style programme on the Home Service with the title 'Home This Afternoon'. With jutting jaw and steely stare, Bob was not always popular with his fellow producers in BH, but he was known to be an 'ideas man' with a staunchly independent spirit. He was also a great believer in the concept of real local radio and involving the community in that concept.

The interview went well enough, and Bob was particularly interested in my hospital radio work and association with a Football League club. Unbeknown to me, he was looking for someone to take over the sports output on the new station, and my knowledge of the game and proven ability at match commentating clearly impressed him.

Add to this the fact that I was comfortable in front of a microphone, familiar with the Brighton area and genuinely enthusiastic about the local radio experiment, and Mr. Gunnell obviously decided that 'Henty' was worth a second interview. This took place 12 days later on Wednesday, 26th July, 1967, and while it went equally well, there was no offer on the table at the end and certainly no way of telling whether I had beaten the odds and landed what could only be described as a plum job in broadcasting.

Meantime, of course, Sylvia was having to adjust to a totally new life-style at home in Raynes Park with a two-month-old baby and, for me, life at West London Air Terminal continued with my two closest colleagues intrigued to know what I was getting up to with the BBC. What could I tell them? Nothing with any certainty. That is, until the fateful phone call came through to my press office extension.

'Mr. Henty? Oh, hello Mr. Henty – this is Bob Gunnell's secretary at the BBC. He's asked me to tell you that you've been accepted as a programme assistant at BBC Radio Brighton, probably starting towards the end of . . . Hello Mr. Henty – did you get that ? It's Bob Gu . . .'

On this occasion, to say that I was gobsmacked would be entirely 100 per cent accurate. To start with I thought the call might have been a hoax

– after all, I had nothing in writing. But the moment I realised that it was genuine, and that I had been chosen out of hundreds of applicants – many of whom actually worked already for the BBC – well, utter astonishment was a fair description of my reaction that morning as I replaced the telephone. Confirmation soon arrived when our information girl, Liz, came into the office with a cutting from the *Brighton Gazette* dated Friday, 11th August, 1967.

The headline read 'THEIR STATION IN LIFE' and listed John Henty 'a journalist with BEA who has worked with local radio stations in the United States', alongside local man, Keith Slade 'well known as an amateur producer and lecturer on drama', Hylda Bamber 'who has spent four and a half years in local radio in New Zealand', Mike Matthews, another broadcaster 'with experience in New Zealand' and former local teacher Christopher Jones, who 'will specialise in educational programmes'.

The newspaper announcement was the first time I learned of my future colleagues. I still had no written confirmation of the appointment and – worse – I had not even handed in my notice to Bill Simpson.

How would he react to the news that one of his team was off to the south coast to be a broadcaster on an experimental local radio station?

24

B ill's reaction to my stunning news was typical of the man I had grown to admire over five exciting years with the state airline. Despite the fact that the only indication we both had of my appointment was a newspaper cutting and an 'out of the blue' telephone conversation, he was genuinely enthusiastic for me and said that he had always regarded me as a frustrated broadcaster biding my time in the press office. Now the opportunity had finally arrive, he was certain I had made the right decision – and the BBC too.

'I'll miss the Henty Pies though, he added with that charming smile of his – and meant it.

Funnily enough, I had more difficulty persuading my parents in Croydon that the appointment was a good career move. My father, whose inherent worrying had probably caused his stroke when I was in America in 1960, appeared philosophical at the news, but mum was not happy and had to be patiently prompted by Sylvia into believing that I was not heading out into the North Sea to reprise my role as a pirate – of gramophone records as opposed to Penzance. Ah, John lad!

Once she did realise that BBC Radio Brighton would not be broadcasting from a rowing boat anchored three miles off the Palace Pier, Mrs. Henty became more enthusiastic.

'Will we be able to hear you in Croydon?'she asked.

'Definitely not, mum – unless the winds blowing in the right direction. Anyway, we're only broadcasting on VHF or FM, so the chances are remote, I'm afraid.'

'Never mind dear, I told you it would pay off if you spoke nicely . . . Another portion of trifle? I made it specially . . .'

In the next three months Sylvia and I spent a number of weekends in my old home in south Croydon with Andrew because we now faced yet another house move, this time down to Sussex by the sea. With an on-air date scheduled for St Valentine's day 1968, Manager, Bob Gunnell, insisted that everyone should be living in the editorial area by Christmas 1967. We soon sold the Raynes Park house – making 50 quid into the bargain – and intensified our search to the east and west of Brighton.

Shoreham-by-Sea appealed, and an estate agent friend, John, found us a new property within walking distance of the mainline railway station and close to the open-spaces of Buckingham Park north of the A27. The 'heaval' was considerably 'up' at this time, and our faithful VW Beetle was more than often packed to the gunwhales (appropriately enough) as we journeyed down the A23 between Raynes Park and Buckingham Park. Andrew was only months old, remember, but took to the turmoil remarkably well – despite experiencing German measles even before we had departed London SW20.

I've always thought watches were normally presented to departing members of staff (especially railway employees) on the occasion of their retirement, after 40 years of faithful whistle-blowing activity at Paddington Station. The timepiece that Bill Simpson handed to me at my leaving party was different, though. It was an Omega stopwatch inscribed with the words: 'To John From Friends at B.E.A' and, as I was soon to discover, it would prove to be a vital piece of equipment in my new broadcasting career. I still have that watch today, and I still use it – although now it is largely employed to prevent me rabbiting on when giving talks to various groups around the country.

I left BEA on a Friday and joined the BBC two days later on Monday, 25th September, 1967, when I presented myself at the Langham – a building immediately opposite Broadcasting House where the Local Radio Training Unit had been hastily set-up.

A mock studio was in place, incorporating a broadcasting desk which allowed a presenter to 'self-operate' – in other words, play in his own records and tape inserts and link to alternative networks or the radio car as an outside source. In 1967 this was revolutionary stuff and not immediately welcomed by the traditionalists across the road. Mind you, they had their own broadcasting breakthrough to cope with this particular autumn, and we were there to see – and hear – it happen.

The arrival of Radio 1 with Tony Blackburn spinning 'Flowers In The Rain' by The Move on the morning of Saturday, 30th September, was exciting stuff, and I can remember the upbeat mood of everybody on our course the following Monday with Radios 2, 3 and 4 also going their own individual ways. We all felt that radio was definitely the place to be.

This confidence was boosted by visits to Broadcasting House during our training, and I can vividly remember sitting in the 'World At One' operations room and watching the portly William Hardcastle in his shirt-sleeves and braces handle a frenetic edition of the lunchtime news programme. On our side of the glass, I noted particularly the producer's assistant desperately doing sums with her stopwatch in hand while another older woman was literally biting her fingernails down to the quick. The pressure was enormous, but others in that tense room, attempting to re-assure me, suggested that it was 'just another day'.

Maybe, but I was almost relieved to return to the Langham and our little bit of local broadcasting history. Learning to handle the new desk was quite a challenge for all of us, and one visiting *Guardian* journalist even suggested that an octopus would be better placed to deal with the numerous knobs, 'pots' and switches on the control panel. For the broadcasting beginners amongst us – and I was certainly not alone – the experience was perhaps akin to learning how to drive a car.

One particular manoeuvre proved to be exceptionally difficult, and this was the occasion when linking into a taped item in the studio. A remote start on the sizeable tape machines worked well, but to operate it one had to close the microphone channel (or 'pot') first. If one failed to do this the tape machine would start with a loud mechanical 'clunk' and this would be heard on air.

The secret was to close the microphone fader before opening the tape fader – a bit like engaging clutch before attempting to change gear. The movements had to be synchronised, and it was devilish difficult to do in the early days, resulting in some rather unprofessional moments – especially during the trial programmes we were asked to create.

Then there was the whole business of editing tape, using a chinagraph pencil and specially-made razor blades; Uher tape recorders and interviewing techniques; the writing of news bulletins and cue material; and how to achieve correct sound levels. It was a challenging time for everyone, even the more seasoned broadcasters among us, and I was certainly helped along and positively encouraged by one of my future colleagues, Mike Matthews.

Mike was bright, breezy and occasionally brash with it, but, my goodness, he enjoyed broadcasting, and it was this spirit of enjoyment that he instilled into me right from the start. Radio should be fun, he reckoned, and his devil-may-care attitude helped me through those early days to dispel self-doubt and the occasional moments of despair. Anyway, the local radio unit at the Langham was no place for despair in October 1967. Panic? Perhaps. Periodic palpitations? Possibly . . . but despair? Nah!

We all knew that this was the start of something BIG in broadcasting and the experimental nature of it only served to heighten the very real sense of adventure we all felt. 'We' were a motley crew, too. There were BBC types, engineering 'bods', old hands at the broadcasting game and newcomers like myself with perhaps only hospital radio experience to fall back on.

We came from all walks of life and from many different parts of the United Kingdom. On my course – or certainly around the time of my course – I remember a very attractive and vivacious young woman who was wowing all the fellows with her enthusiasm and outgoing personality. Kate Adie, of course, was destined for great things in the years ahead and even became a neighbour of mine in Brighton for a short time in the 1970s. At the Langham, she was a breath of fresh air and good fun, too. We are still in touch to this day, and she may be surprised (even alarmed) to know that then, from afar, I fancied her like mad. From afar, Sylvia! As in 'at a very great distance'.

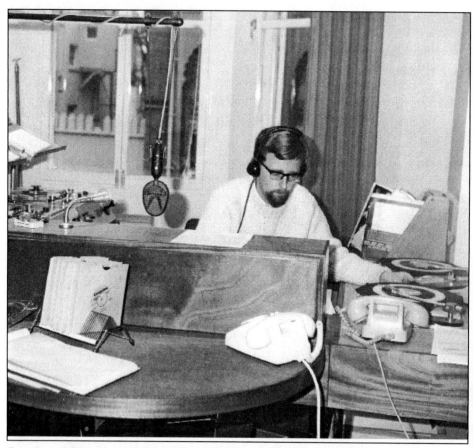

Fat Boy Slim eat your heart out! The early days at Radio Brighton were exciting times, and local broadcasting was very much do-it-yourself. This is Studio One at Marlborough Place, 1969.

This was also a time to get better acquainted with other members of the Radio Brighton team. Apart from the five producers, there were three station assistants, all women, and one general station assistant by the name of Michael Quinion. The manager had a very clear picture of what our future roles would involve once we arrived on the south coast. Hylda Bamber was to be responsible for women's interests with a daily morning programme called 'Coffee Break', Keith Slade was to concentrate on the local arts scene, Mike Matthews a mix of general programmes, Chris Jones education and John Henty . . . ? General programmes with an emphasis on sport and leisure pursuits.

The BBC had acquired a former hotel premises opposite the northern gates of Brighton's Royal Pavilion – Marlborough Place – to set up shop, and while this could not have been more central, it was to present our engineers, Ted Castle and George Orchard, with major technical problems, all the studios having to be located on four different floors.

This meant that when the broadcasting team finally reported for duty in Brighton, it was to discover that there were no studios operational and everyone was crammed into one production office. It was certainly a good way to get to know your colleagues, and in the true spirit of local radio everyone mucked in, sharing desks and telephones, and consuming copious cups of coffee.

At this point, Sylvia, Andrew and I were living temporarily with my parents, and I commuted on a daily basis from East Croydon down to Brighton – a mere 45 minutes or so by train. That is, when it wasn't snowing in Sussex and, my goodness, didn't it snow, children, in the first few days of December 1967. Freak weather maybe, but what a golden opportunity for Radio Brighton to prove its true worth to a doubting community.

Typically, Bob Gunnell grabbed the opportunity with both hands and then it was simply a question of 'all hands on deck', Wellington boots, a temporary studio in the Royal Pavilion and . . . no John Henty.

I was snow-bound in Croydon, cursing my luck.

25

They say 'There's no business like snow business,' don't they? Well, something along those lines, and this was certainly true of Bob Gunnell's fledgling radio station when the early winter weather decided to turn very nasty in December 1967. Once the move to go on air early had been approved and a suitable radio frequency found, Bob and his team leapt into action and the town of Brighton suddenly discovered its own voice for the very first time.

Regional radio had never been like this. Local people soon realised that Radio Brighton was talking directly to them and, with its 'snow desk', bringing news of school closures, emergency shopping arrangements, help for older listeners and the vital travel and traffic information as it happened – all this from a temporary studio two months before the official scheduled opening and with depleted staff numbers. I was certainly not the only person to have been stranded outside the editorial area when the snows came.

The message, however, was loud and clear, even if the transmitted signal at the time was not up to much. Radio Brighton had a role to play in the community and was here to stay. The local daily paper cautiously echoed this theme though ever conscious of the fact that the BBC in town represented competition to its own previously unassailable position.

When I finally did get back to Marlborough Place through the sludge and rain, I noticed that the mood among my colleagues had changed markedly. There was now almost an impatience to get on air as soon as possible, and a desperate desire to start working in the shiny new studios. Those who had been involved with the emergency broadcasts were still buzzing with that sense of urgency, and their renewed enthusiasm rubbed off on the rest of us. To hell with Christmas: let's jump to 14th February, 1968!

And that's what we shall do – to St. Valentine's day, a cold and misty Wednesday and an early evening start for BBC Radio Brighton on 88.1 Mhz VHF. Keith Slade had already recorded the opening programme which starred, amongst others, Dame Flora Robson, Dora Bryan and Laurence Olivier, all local residents. Hylda Bamber told newspaper reporters that she was planning to spend the night in Marlborough Place to ensure that she was awake to open the station the following morning.

Mike Matthews played the first record request for firemen on duty at close-by Preston Circus, and John Henty . . . ? I climbed aboard the brand new radio car with engineer George Orchard and prepared to make the station's first outside broadcast from the top of the town's highest building. It seemed like a good idea at the planning stage, but remember that this was evening time in the winter and, yes, it was misty, *very* misty. So when I got to the top of the building – Sussex Heights, just off the seafront, midway between the two piers – and walked out onto the roof area with the janitor, I immediately noticed . . . nothing.

It was dark, silent and there was no view whatsoever to speak of. And, of course, that was my whole purpose for being there – to speak of the wonderful views to our curious listeners down below. Add to this the fact that I was using a radio microphone with a poor signal for my very first broadcast, and that I could hardly hear any of the station's output over my headphones, and you have a reporter's nightmare.

Not so long ago, for the very first time, I heard a recording of that hysterical – sorry, historical – moment and, to my credit, the item worked because I was honest enough to admit that there was absolutely nothing to see. It would have been a wonderful view, I suggested, if the fog cleared but, meantime, let's meet the man whose job it is to look after this prestigious building. Fortunately, he entered into the spirit of the thing and my two minutes of glory were soon over, and I handed back to Mike in the studio.

No time for congratulations, though: we then belted off to fulfil my role as sports producer by visiting indoor nets in Hove where a few members of the Sussex County Cricket Club were practising. This multi-faceted side of our work was to prove very demanding and typical of the way things had to operate in the early stages of local radio. While each programme assistant had individual responsibilities, we also read the news (which was then provided by a news agency), performed continuity announcing through the day, put the radio car away in a local garage at night and often opened-up the station early the following morning.

There were daily news magazines to present, plus two editions of the breakfast show 'Coastwise'. And then there were all the weekend programmes to consider as well – with outside broadcasts a regular feature on a Saturday morning at midday, and specialist programmes for gardeners, watersports enthusiasts and motorists. No wonder the record 'If I Only Had Time' by John Rowles was so popular with the broadcasting team in those first frenzied weeks.

After the excitement of the opening night, Hylda did wake up the following morning to start the first full day of broadcasting, and this included her own half-hour 'Coffee Break' programme. I had until the next day, Friday, to prepare for my debut as sports presenter, and the programme organiser, David Waine, joined me in putting the 'Sports Parade' show together.

Of course, the remarkable thing about all the programming at this time was that we had absolutely no guidelines whatsoever to follow. There were no other local stations to observe or emulate, and we were therefore obliged to adhere to our own instincts. David and I were clearly influenced by sports coverage on national radio and decided to concentrate much of our effort on reporting the fortunes of the only Football League side in Sussex, Brighton and Hove Albion.

To help us do this we approached a local newspaper journalist, Jack Arlidge, and he jumped at the chance of covering matters out at the Goldstone ground. Jack was a delightful person, very much from the old school of sports journalism, and he rapidly developed an idiosyncratic style which was perfect for local radio. He started all his reports by addressing 'Sussex sports fans' and regularly turned up at the studio on a Friday evening with a bemused sporting celebrity who'd probably never heard of BBC Radio Brighton.

Jack was there on that first Friday night and brought with him a couple of local athletes who were preparing for the forthcoming Olympic Games. My sports 'team' as such was mainly made up of keen freelance individuals, most of whom had little or no broadcasting experience. Our boxing coverage was provided by a postal worker, Derek Leney, athletics was the responsibility of a certain Reg Hook and a solicitor, Stanley Allen, was to lead our cricket commentary team in the summer months ahead at the County Ground, Hove. All of them offered their services for practically nothing as my sports budget was pitifully inadequate, but the experience it gave them of working behind a microphone was invaluable (I would say that, wouldn't I?), and there were soon plenty of local sporting enthusiasts who wanted to join us at Marlborough Place.

To tap this clear potential, David and I agreed to insert an advertisement in the *Evening Argus* which invited anyone with an interest in sport – and particularly local sport – to come for an audition and learn more about our planned coverage of the area. The response, not surprisingly, was very encouraging, and no one seemed to be put off by the fact that there was no money in it.

David and I shared the auditions between us, and a simple microphone test was conducted in the tiny BBC studio housed in the Royal Pavilion. Our number one priority was not to find the next Brian Johnston or Moore, although as it happens that is almost what we did do. No, our search at that time was to find enthusiasts – people who were prepared to spend long Saturday afternoons on wet and windy non-league football grounds and report back to the studio via the only public telephone situated in the corner of the club bar. People who could get excited about table tennis, bowls, darts and, yes, croquet even – BIG in Sussex!

They would all have a place on Radio Brighton's sports output, and eventually we did have specialist programmes from 'On The Green' with Fred Bates (honest!), to 'Double Top' with news of the lively Sussex Darts League. 'Sunday Soccer' was another rare offering which quickly developed a cult-following for half-an-hour or so on Monday evenings. It was produced and presented entirely by a team of volunteers, most of whom had never broadcast before. For my part, I suggested a jazzy signature tune (all programmes had to have a signature tune) and then cheerfully left the 'Likely Lads' to get on with it – and, believe me, they did, with match reports, player interviews in the studio and all the results, which seemed to go on and on forever.

And so too did the auditions in the Royal Pavilion and Marlborough Place, but David and I were soon narrowing down the short-list of potential team-players. Among them was the name of a rather laid-back character in his early twenties who said that he was 'something' in insurance on the south coast (never really did find out what . . .) and was interested in all sports and particularly football.

Fortunately he didn't try to sell us insurance, but he certainly sold himself well enough and the name was quickly added to our list. Even then I thought it had a good sporting ring to it.

Desmond Lynam? Let's give him a try . . .

26

I suppose it's almost inevitable. When someone makes the 'big time' after a more than modest start in the broadcasting basement of local radio there will always be those who determine that they alone 'discovered' the debutant. Where Des Lynam is concerned I make no such claims. He was clearly a natural broadcaster who was comfortable in front of a microphone and happiest when talking sport.

What I was able to do in those early days was to encourage him with various sporting assignments which he accomplished with a professional flair – and all for a couple of quid a time. On one occasion, for example, he turned a straightforward tribute to veteran Albion striker Alex Dawson into a six-minute feature which included a phone conversation with Michael Parkinson. That was flair.

No, if anybody discovered Desmond Lynam during his time at Radio Brighton, it was the man himself. All I did was to make him believe in his own ability and, more importantly, do something with it.

Apart from self-belief, I like to think that Des also learned to introduce a spot of humour into his sporting approach when working at Marlborough Place. Certainly we never took sport too seriously, and there were numerous occasions in the studio when pressure of work produced spontaneous laughter. One Saturday evening I was reading out the Sussex League football results during a particularly hairy half-hour of 'Sports Desk' when I came across – was it Patcham 1 Horsham YMCA14? Unfortunately, I added a pencilled note from the result-taker which read '. . . and our correspondent tells me that the Patcham keeper had a good game.' This amused me somewhat, and as I read it my voice wobbled and I simply could not prevent myself from laughing. A lot! Worse was to follow because other contributors around the table in the studio also started to laugh and the whole thing got completely out of control. In the end, the studio assistant next door brought up our signature tune on disc and effectively closed the programme early.

Des wasn't there on that occasion, but would have heard about it. I know he also tells the story of our coverage of an evening football league cup game between first division Wolverhampton Wanderers and Brighton and Hove Albion in the autumn of 1969. David Waine and I agreed to provide reports live from the Goldstone Ground, using the radio car which

Sharing a joke with the Barron Knights during a typical outside broadcast on Brighton's famous Palace Pier.

was parked in the players' car park. Almost unbelievably, we had not secured our seats in the cramped press section, and when we arrived, it was to discover that there was no room for the 'newcomers'. Embarrassing!

We moved down into two vacant seats just in front of the press and everything seemed OK until just after kick-off when the owners of the two seats arrived. Muriel and Norman Thurgur were lifetime Seagull supporters who'd been held up in traffic on their journey from nearby Southwick (over 30,000 fans attended the game that night) and we were in their sacred seats. More embarrassment!

David and I muttered our apologies and shuffled, heads-down, along the line of equally indignant home supporters towards the gangway where we halted and turned our agitated attention once again to the cup tie. What we didn't know was that during the seat-shifting scenario, Wolves had scored a sneaky goal which had been greeted around the ground by deafening silence – so deafening that neither of us latched onto the fact that something pretty significant had happened. The midlanders were a goal ahead.

Not according to our reports throughout the entire first 45-minutes of the game, though. We merrily and obliviously chuntered on about Brighton's great performance and correctly reported their two goals through striker Alan Gilliver and stocky Eddie Spearritt. Two-nil to the Seasiders at half-time, according to reporters Waine and Henty.

It was a police constable outside the ground who eventually blew the whistle on us by telephoning the studio with the horrendous news that Radio Brighton was relaying the wrong score. You can imagine our reaction when we were passed this information minutes later – and even

Our 'studio' at the Goldstone Ground.

to this day, neither David Waine or I can recall how we got out of a commentator's nightmare. Perhaps it was by using the aforementioned humour, but I doubt whether Albion supporters at home would have been amused. And the final score: Brighton and Hove Albion 2 Wolverhampton Wanderers 3. At least, I think it was . . .

As a result of this debacle in which he was personally involved, David, as programme organiser, agreed with me that we urgently needed our own broadcasting position at the ground. Negotiations were started with Albion's management, and they approved our plan to erect a studio (well, garden shed actually) on the terracing to the left of the main stand.

From what I recall, the wooden structure was raised off the ground by scaffolding, had no sound insulation at all and smelt strongly of creosote and coconut matting. Members of the sports team helped with the construction, and I even ended up fitting one or two of the ready-prepared glass windows. I did think to myself at the time – can you imagine Angus McKay, producer of the national 'Sports Report' on Radio 2, doing this ? It didn't seem wildly feasible.

With our own studio wired for sound, coverage of all matters Brighton and Hove Albion improved enormously and prompted me to introduce a new programme into the weekend schedules called, appropriately enough, the 'Goldstone Sound'. This was a live broadcast from the new 'studio', which went on air one hour before kick-off at every first team home game.

In addition to being part of Radio Brighton's Saturday afternoon output, the pacy mix of speech and music was also relayed over the tinny tannoy to early arrivals at the football ground. It was very much pre-match entertainment based on my previous experience in south London, with player interviews, news headlines, record requests and even weather and traffic reports – run-of-the mill-stuff today, but then it was a first for any football club in the country and it also served to introduce local radio to a large number of people who did not have access to the station's FM output.

Remember, when BBC Radio Brighton first went on air it was on VHF only and the medium wave facility followed much later in September 1972. With the 'Goldstone Sound' we were able to get our message across to a new audience, and the modest wooden studio helped us to provide a greatly improved coverage for all games. Even Des found himself sharing the cramped facilities from time to time, and I can certainly recall seeing him in one corner practising commentary skills into a portable tape recorder.

This was not his only strength, by the way, and the good-natured humour of the man was to emerge when he collaborated with me to produce and present a short satirical series which we called (somewhat mysteriously) 'How Lunchtime It Is!' Typical of the innovative and inventive nature of local radio at that time, the 15-minute comedy show was almost thrown together by a group of us in our – well, I was going to say spare time, except that we never really had any.

Des and I wrote the script separately (and even that was unusual, because scripts were practically unheard of), the cast of four or five would have a brief rehearsal in somebody's house and then we'd record the end product in whatever studio was available and mostly late at night.

It was a very short series, and Des and I remember a Christmas edition which was ingeniously titled 'How Yuletide It Is!' and featured a doctored version of a Christmas carol and a scurrilous sketch involving a motto-manufacturer of Christmas Crackers called E.I. Adio. 'That Was The Week That Was' it wasn't, but we enjoyed putting it together and the unique opportunity it gave us of writing something for radio which would actually get on air.

In similar vein I introduced local radio's first travel programme, 'Travel Bag', and devised a half-hour documentary called 'Away' which followed a footballer and two stalwart supporters on their separate journeys to an away fixture in the north of England. Inevitably, the team was Brighton and Hove Albion. The supporters? Muriel and Norman Thurgur – remember them ? And the away ground? Spotlands, the home of Rochdale FC.

Meantime, Des was getting more and more radio experience under his belt but, wisely, still retained the day job in insurance which involved servicing clients along the south coast. To this end, in December 1969 I sold him my much-loved red VW beetle – yet it was only four months later that Sylvia and I were invited to a splendid party at a French restaurant in Brighton to celebrate his landing a job with the Radio 2 sports unit in Broadcasting House, London.

Weeks earlier, we'd both had to persuade the guy that the job was worth going for and could be the start of bigger and better things. On Saturday, 18th April, 1970, surrounded by friends and fellow broadcasters, Desmond Lynam needed no further persuasion. He was on his way and knew it. Cheers, Des!

27

Up in our loft – somewhere – I have two or three autograph albums which contain some pretty impressive names, ranging from school chums of mine in south Croydon to Crystal Palace footballers and numerous English county cricket sides. It all started when my mum and I attended a theatrical garden party at the Oval cricket ground in south London just after the war.

The stars certainly turned out on this money-raising occasion and 11-year-old John Henty, armed only with a pencil and small autograph book, was in his element. West End artists included Basil Radford and Naunton Wayne, Dame Lilian Braithwaite, the American star Dolores Gray, who was appearing in 'Oklahoma', and the eccentric Hermione Gingold. A young Richard Dimbleby was covering the event for BBC television and I even cornered the suave Ivor Novello as he chatted with the singer Olive Gilbert over a glass of wine – or was it a cup of tea?

The pencilled names are still there today alongside the likes of Frankie Laine, Sir Donald Bradman and the entire cast of Radio's 'Much Binding In The Marsh'. It was my schoolboy hobby, and I even encouraged others with an article in the Crusader magazine (a Christian organization for boys) which was my first-ever published work.

By the time I'd joined the BBC, the albums were relegated to a cardboard box – which is a pity in a way, because at Radio Brighton there were numerous opportunities for meeting celebrities on air. Imagine my delight, for example, when arts producer Keith Slade asked me to visit Dame Flora Robson in her Brighton home in order to record a poem she had been sent to commemorate Remembrance Day.

Dame Flora was a well known figure in the town and lived in a delightful terraced house close by the ancient St. Nicholas church. After the brief recording, which required a couple of 'takes' as she was suffering from a cold, I was offered a glass of port (very civilised) in her comfortable lounge. We spent the next hour discussing her remarkable career, which included working in Hollywood with the flamboyant Errol Flynn. She liked him a lot, she told me, and – bearing in mind his playboy reputation – it was no surprise to learn that the feeling was mutual, if short-lived.

Fascinating stuff, of course, but the tape recorder remained off, for that was not the purpose of my visit and I got a distinct impression that Dame

Flora was just happy to talk with someone away from the microphones. I was privileged to have this private conversation and resisted the temptation to ask for her autograph.

Other celebrities for one reason or another found their way onto the airwaves in Brighton by visiting the Marlborough Place studios. Lenny Henry popped in to use the loo on a Saturday afternoon and ended up as my guest. George Melly dropped by after visiting an exhibition of surreal art in the nearby Brighton Museum. He stayed for at least half-an-hour – unfazed and unannounced.

One guy burst into the first floor studio – again on a Saturday afternoon – and genuinely left me well and truly gobsmacked. American singer/ songwriter Gerard Kenny had been appearing in the town with my favourite Goon, Spike Milligan. Gerard, who wrote major hits for Barry Manilow and the theme tune to 'Minder' on television, is one helluva character and (as a modest tribute to his enormous talent) I played a track from his album 'All For A Dream' to open my show.

'Son of a Song and Dance Man' is an autobiographical, up-tempo number which really got things off to a good start, and I mentioned on air to sports presenter Mike Buckingham how much I'd enjoyed Gerard's contribution to Spike's mayhem out at the Gardner Arts Centre midweek. Meantime, in an off-licence somewhere in Hove, our conversation was overheard by the man himself, and apparently, Gerard demanded to know what radio station he was listening to and how he could find a taxi to take him there. Ten minutes later – to my amazement and the utter astonishment of 'Buckers' – in rushed Gerard Kenny to plonk himself noisily into the guest chair and tell me all about his dad and the vaudeville days in New York City. The Milligan anecdotes were pretty good too, and I have to say that Gerard must go down as one of my all-time favourite interviewees.

And talking of vaudeville, when old time variety was revived on Brighton's Palace Pier for a summer season in the early seventies, it gave me the golden opportunity to interview such notables as Leslie Sarony, Elsie and Doris Waters who lived locally, Sandy Powell and Mr. 'Rubberneck' himself, Nat Jackley – true professionals all of them, but sadly the show 'Music Hall At the Palace' did not pull in the punters and effectively ended live entertainment on the pier forever.

The theatre was closed and then pulled down – to be replaced by slot machines and the like. Say no more. Radio Brighton, too, was threatened with closure towards the end of its experimental life, and I came up with an emotive campaign which almost literally touched people's hearts . . .

28

There is absolutely no doubt about it: after only a couple of years or so the future of BBC local radio in the United Kingdom was very much in the balance. Former athlete Christopher Chattaway, now a Conservative MP and responsible for the expansion of all forms of radio, was under some pressure from his own party to give the green light to commercial radio interests, while the Labour opposition was largely opposed to this and favoured the modest expansion of the existing BBC network.

At BBC Radio Brighton we were not unaware of this on-going debate and the uncertainty about our future employment. As I described at the beginning, Sylvia and I had moved, with Andrew, from our Buckingham Mews home in Shoreham to a new development of houses in the very centre of Brighton, minutes from the radio station. I'd spotted the building work in Kew Street on my weary way home one evening and we were able to reserve an end-of-terrace property which had a through lounge, two bedrooms, a small patio garden and an integral garage. It also had what was for us in the summer of 1971 a terrifying price – a little over £9,000.

Taking on a mortgage at any time is a daunting process, and it was not helped by one building society turning us down because they weren't 'confident of the long-term potential of a town-centre property in Brighton'. This was short-sighted in the extreme, and I made this point in a terse letter to the company in which I described their treatment of us as 'shabby' – which may give you a clue as to which specific society I was alluding to. Now, if they'd said 'No, sorry, we're not happy with your long-term job prospects in Brighton' then I might have understood their reasoning.

It would have been a fair argument. We were under pressure at Marlborough Place and my fear, shared by the station management, was that very few of our listeners – however loyal – fully appreciated how close we were to being switched-off for good – it could have been that dramatic. So I devised a publicity ploy to increase people's awareness of our plight which involved a pretty nurse and some carefully chosen words. Manager Gunnell approved

We pointed out, on air, that Radio Brighton, which had opened on St. Valentine's day in 1968, was at the very heart of the local community and that 'heart' was beating bravely and strongly. But what if it suddenly stopped ? What if it was not allowed to carry-on doing its vital job in the Sussex editorial area? Dead air indeed!

To illustrate this we required the sound of a healthy heart – so that meant excluding most members of the broadcasting team. It would also need to be recorded by our engineers in a peaceful setting and with a photographer on hand for publicity purposes. A local hospital, Southlands, was chosen and a young member of the nursing staff pin-pointed to provide the coronary accompaniment. Station engineer Ted Castle took along his most sensitive sound equipment, and a freelance on the station, John Williams, who just happened to have a decent camera, came along for the ride.

Fixing a miniature microphone to an area not far removed from a delightfully pert bosom was Ted's technical task for the afternoon, and he did it with some considerable aplomb. All the while our photographer clicked away and was clearly impressed by what he did or did not see because within weeks he was 'going steady' with our Miss Heartbeat and ultimately married the girl in a swirl of publicity. Who said romance is dead?

The resulting boom-boom of the future Mrs. William's heart was built into Radio Brighton's distinctive identification or 'call-sign' sequence and broadcast, on the hour, with the message 'Radio Brighton at the heart of our community', or words to that effect. And the message worked. Listeners wrote to their members of Parliament, letters were aimed at national newspapers and a fair amount of lobbying was achieved by the broadcasters themselves.

Commercial radio would be coming, Chattaway announced to the House of Commons, but meantime BBC local radio was given a thumbs-up and the go-ahead to open more stations. We were 'legit' at last. It was a very good feeling indeed, and pleasing to know that my heart idea had played a small but significant part in the overall campaign. Like Bill Simpson at BEA before him, Bob Gunnell appreciated the Henty 'ideas', and I presented him with another ambitious one in the autumn of 1971 – a proposal that would take me back to the USA (albeit only for a couple of weeks) – to middle-America and a small community a short drive from mighty Detroit City in the state of Michigan. It would also allow me to visit Motown's studios there and meet a real pop idol, Smokey Robinson.

29

During my short spell on the *Croydon Advertiser* 10 years previously I had written a series of features based on other Croydons around the world. This was largely achieved by spending long sessions in the town library and writing off numerous letters to tourist offices and local newspapers covering the relevant areas overseas. I did suggest to my editor at the time, Geoff Collard, that it would be even better if I was able to actually visit some of the communities – five Croydons in Australia and two in New Zealand, for example – but he wasn't sold on the idea.

However, I did travel to a couple of English Croydons. One was in the west country and another was a small hamlet not far removed from the city of Cambridge, but it wasn't quite the approach I had originally envisaged. Fascinating stuff though, and the series proved popular when it came out and provoked a fair amount of useful correspondence on the letters page.

'So Bob,' I said, addressing Radio Brighton's station manager, 'How about forming a radio link with another Brighton, preferably in America – one that has its own radio station? I have a contact in the United States Travel Service in London who might help us set it up and would probably arrange to get me out there.' When he heard that it wouldn't cost the station any money, Bob became interested and told me to pursue the matter and report back to him, which I did in double-quick time.

The USTS contact also liked the idea and nominated Brighton in Michigan as a likely participant in the innovative scheme. Contact was made with the city through the chamber of commerce and I was offered accommodation with their executive director, Art Schuman, who had recently retired from running a business downtown. He lived with his wife Verna in a pleasant, typically American homestead and knew everything and everybody associated with the growing community.

It all sounded very encouraging from this side of the pond – certainly Bob thought so. A Pan Am flight was fixed, my UK broadcasting duties were covered for a couple of weeks in October and I was even invited to contribute a guest column or two for the local *Argus* newspaper in Michigan. Yes, remarkably, Brighton, England is not the only city with an *Argus* newspaper – and there were other coincidences too. I also asked Art to see whether he could fix me up with a visit to the famous Tamla Motown Studios in Detroit – some 40 miles or so down the inter-state highway. This was a tall order for a retired gentleman more likely to enjoy Jim Reeves than Martha, but he made a few phone calls and cheerily confirmed that we would motor down to Detroit together at some point during my 14-day stay. No promises but . . .

For me the whole operation was a challenge, and in those two breath-taking weeks I covered every aspect of contemporary life in Middle America with a Uher tape recorder and a battered Rolleicord camera. Let's face it, 'You're welcome!' is an Americanism that all too easily rolls off the transatlantic tongue, but in Brighton, Michigan, during my stay in 1971, it was frequently said and sincerely meant as I journeyed from high school to high church. There were meetings to address, articles to write for both *Argus* newspapers and additionally, on a day-to-day basis, I reported back live to home base – Radio Brighton in Sussex. I put together programme inserts for the women's morning magazine 'Coffee Break', I attended a high school American football game for the sports output and even visited General Motors proving grounds outside the city for a road-testing item used in the motoring magazine 'At The Wheel'. It was all invigorating stuff, and I have never felt quite so fulfilled and creative on an overseas assignment as I did on this one.

The journey into Detroit was special, too. Art, who must have been well into his seventies, drove an enormous automatic Pontiac in style down the highway and deposited me outside the Motown building with a warning not to wander off on my own. A dangerous city? Yes, and violent with it, but dynamic, too – a proud city with a style and panache which I immediately liked.

Motown at 2457 Woodward Avenue was a modest-looking, almost tenement-like structure which I could easily have missed without Art Schuman's local knowledge. He'd arranged for me to meet the record company's public relations manager, and probably told her that I was one of England's top-rated BBC radio presenters. Whatever it was he said over the phone, Barbara Tarvid was waiting for me once I had negotiated several electronic security doors to get into the ground floor reception area.

I had expected to meet a black woman, because at that time the Motown sound was synonymous with a style of inner-city music created solely by black musicians – a young Stevie Wonder, Marvin Gaye, Smokey Robinson and groups like the Four Tops, the Temptations and the Supremes. I was surprised then to find that Ms Tarvid was in fact white, probably in her thirties and very unassuming. She was no doubt surprised to discover that I was not a top British 'Jock.'. Despite these discrepancies, we got on well and moved up to her impressively cluttered office in the heart of the building.

Here, over coffee, Barbara gave me a run-down of all the Motown artists working for the organisation in Detroit and told me to watch out for a new label 'Rare Earth' and an up and coming group, the Jacksons. She played me the Supremes' current hit 'Nathan Jones' and also suggested that the company might be moving its entire operation across America to the West Coast – a move too far, she hinted, and certainly not popular with a good number of the Detroit devotees.

Remarkably, she then invited me to make my own tour of the building, and this was how I came across creative administrator Hank Cosby, who I found seated at a keyboard trying out one or two chord sequences, or riffs. Hank told me that he had worked with the young Stevie Wonder and was responsible for his first major hit 'Finger Tips'; then came 'Love Child' and 'My Cherie Amour'. I soon realised that I was talking to a Motown legend – yet here he was in a bleak rehearsal room, completely on his own and totally unassuming.

On another floor Barbara re-appeared in the company of a smiling guy who greeted me warmly and spoke of his many British fans who had helped to make 'Tears Of A Clown' a massive hit in the United Kingdom. Like everyone I met that day, including one of the Four Tops, Smokey Robinson could not have been more approachable, and I came away from Woodward Avenue greatly impressed by the entire Motown set-up. I understand the building is now a museum devoted to the story of Motown and well-worth a visit if you find yourself – as I did – in dynamic Detroit City. The artists may well be computer-generated now, but the sound will always be the same – sensational.

The two-weeks in Middle America were soon over though, and in no time I was winging my way back to the middle of . . . Brighton, and the day-to-day business of parish pump radio. However, I have to say that my initial enthusiasm for local broadcasting was beginning to diminish, and certainly visiting council estate Moulsecoomb on a Saturday morning OB (outside broadcast) in the pouring rain was no match for a frenzied fortnight in Michigan, USA. No match at all!

True to my nature, what I wanted now was a fresh challenge, and this duly arrived in the form of a six-month attachment to BBC Radio 2 in London where I would read the national news, introduce 'Night Ride' and briefly share Tony Blackburn's Christmas Morning Show on Radio 1. Sublime to the ridiculous? You could say so.

30

The night before my first news-reading stint on Radio 2 I was totally unable to sleep, not even nodding off for the odd few minutes or so. It wasn't the noise of traffic in the centre of town, I assured Sylvia, nor the prospect of catching an early morning train up to London from nearby Brighton station. No, the reason for my restlessness was simply the terrifying awareness that in less than 12 hours I would be handed a news bulletin and expected to address what I saw as the entire . . . . ing nation!

Reaching remote villages on the Sussex/Surrey border with news of Brighton and Hove Albion's latest on-loan signing was one thing. Telling listeners as far apart as St. Austell and Stockholm of a military coup in Guatemala was another. And how do you pronounce the deposed president's name for God's sake ? And what if I overrun the two minutes and then forget to mention the time of the next bulletin? And what . . . ?

Under the circumstances it's a miracle I even got as far as Oxford Circus underground station. The bag of nerves was overflowing on that particular October morning in 1973, and Broadcasting House loomed large on my hesitant horizon. However, once through the famous portal and issued with a temporary security pass, I was warmly welcomed by fellow announcers in their – what I can only describe as locker room on the second floor. The head of presentation, Jimmy Kingsbury, introduced me around and gave me a rota of weekly responsibilities. There was the dapper Robin Boyle of 'Friday Night Is Music Night' fame, a young Colin Berry and an even younger – and more bumptious – Simon Bates.

I soon discovered that Mr Bates was aiming for the big time in broadcasting and practically lived for and on the job. The shipping forecast and 'Night Ride' once a week was not for him. He wanted his own show on Radio 1 and, of course, eventually got it. To be fair to Simon, he was ambitious on my behalf too and, typically, at the Radio 1 Christmas party that year, propelled me in the direction of some radio bigwig who greeted me graciously but was gone within seconds. I want none of this 'hollow-hello' business, I thought to myself, whatever Simple Simon says.

Once I got over the initial shock of that first lunchtime bulletin, the news reading bit became almost routine. For most of the time it originated from a small cubicle which was an integral part of the radio newsroom. As a journalist, I enjoyed this close proximity with 'real reporters', and between the bulletins would often sit alongside copy-takers as the running stories of the day developed.

There were other responsibilities, too. The shipping forecast from another cubby hole was regarded by some as almost a religious ritual. Jimmy Kingsbury – a former announcer himself and a self-styled seafarer – was seemingly obsessed by it. The announcers knew that their target audience was probably heaving about on the high seas north of the Hebrides, but they also knew that a certain Mr Kingsbury in the same building was timing their every utterance and noting the slightest deviation from the prepared script. If the cubicle phone rang within seconds of closing the microphone you knew it would be Cap'n Kingsbury. 'Welcome aboard, sir . . . what did I miss out today?'

Before 24-hour radio became the norm, Radio 2 would normally close down at 2am, and the programme after midnight for two hours was known, among other things, as 'Night Ride' and later 'You And The Night And The Music'. The responsibility for presenting this middle-of-the road, middle-of-the-night mish-mash was ours – the Radio 2 continuity announcers.

For newcomer John Henty it was the opportunity to demonstrate his local radio skills and to break away from the news-reading strait-jacket that fitted so uncomfortably. My first 'Night Ride', then under producer Pam Cox, was on Wednesday, October 10, 1973, and though I say it myself, everything went very well indeed. Jimmy liked it too and even rang, perhaps foolishly, to say that it was the 'Best Night Ride he'd heard for a long time'.

The main reason for his praise was probably that I played the presentation strictly by the book – no flashy introductions, no silly jokes, no talking over records and rigid adherence to the running order. That would all change in the weeks to come, of course, but as I crossed the road between Broadcasting House and the overnight accommodation in the Langham at half past two in the morning, I knew that late night broadcasting was for me. It was impossible to sleep again, but this time for all the right reasons.

Producer Pam was impressed too, as she told me the following morning, and seven days later when I visited the production offices in Charlotte Street she showed me a good number of letters that had been provoked by my 'very proper' presentation. Listeners' letters were a major part of the local radio package, but now there were lengthy communications from people right across the country and within Europe, too. They also included two former girlfriends who clearly couldn't believe their ears as they half-listened to late night radio on a murky Wednesday evening. John Henty? Whatever happened to John Henty? Now they knew, and one even wanted a signed photograph for her two daughters. It was good to be in touch again. Strange, too.

Other duties during my six-month stint in Broadcasting House included covering for Jimmy Young in a lonely basement studio while he chuntered on with his menus and consumer items; laughing at Tony Blackburn's jokes on his Christmas Day programme on Radio1; bashing out the hyped-up headlines on newly introduced Radio 1's 'Newsbeat' and reading the news into Ray Moore's weekend shows. Ray was my favourite broadcaster, and what you heard on the radio was what you got in the staff canteen. He was what I call a one-to-one man. He had the sort of voice and intimate style that seemed to be speaking to you alone.

And if you were alone with Ray, then that was special and a privilege. I would pop into his studio from time to time in the late evening. It was nearly always dimly lit, and between the records we would have what he and I could only describe as a 'natter'. Ray Moore is sadly missed on radio today, but he's certainly not forgotten.

On one Saturday evening following Ray's programme it was my responsibility to close Radio 2 and to remind listeners to forward their clocks by one hour to establish British Summertime. As this meant I too had lost an hours kip in the Langham and was required to be on duty with the shipping forecast soon after 6 a.m on Sunday morning, I decided to stay up and wander the curiously curving corridors of Broadcasting House. Eventually, I ended up in the basement and there – joy of joys – I came across equipment that was clearly used by the sound effects department. For the next half-hour, I crunched up gravel paths, opened and closed numerous doors and pretended I was part of the Goons' entourage in the Camden Theatre all those years ago – no socks filled with canteen custard though.

It was all great fun at the time, but I was ever conscious that I was only on a six-month attachment from Radio Brighton and it would soon be necessary to return to the run-of-the-mill local radio business in Marlborough Place. Pam Cox and her executive producer Cyril Drake were more than happy with my 'Night Ride' presentation and told me so, but Jimmy Kingsbury was a tougher nut to crack and he was the guy who made the decisions.

At the end of February – my final show was on Wednesday, February 27, 1974 – Jimmy bought me a couple of pints of Guinness in the BBC

Club, shook my hand vigorously and said he hoped we would work together in the future. A standard letter followed along similar lines, but of course we never did meet again. He retired and I returned to guest-present 'Night Ride' for Pam on several occasions and, as a freelance, to contribute items to 'You And The Night' etcetera.

Disappointed? Well, this poem summed up my view at the time and was posted on the noticeboard in the presenters' locker room following my departure:

So . . .
I knew there'd be a catch
When they said why not attach
Yourself to London – just to read the national news
After six years of hard flog
By the seaside – as a cog.
'Twas an offer which I just could not refuse.

So . . .
I came to London Town
And don't think I let 'em down,
Did the ships, read the news and played DJ

But . . .
When all is said and done
And you're sent back to Square One
Is it worth it? You may ask, and well you may.

Well . . .
Despite the way it's ended
There are nice folks I've befriended
And to all of them I'd like to bid 'adieu'.
And before I disappear,
I'll state very firmly here . . .
YOU'VE NOT HEARD THE LAST OF HENTY – ONE AND TWO!

Reading the news is one thing I decided, but it's better to be making it or reporting it. Read on . . .

31

When I returned to the airwaves of BBC Radio Brighton in the spring of 1974, Sylvia, Andrew and I had been joined in our end of terrace house in Kew Street by my father, Lionel, who was still suffering the after-effects of his earlier stroke. My mother's death in Croydon at the early age of 63 had been a great shock to all of us, and it soon became clear that Dad was not going to be able to cope on his own in our Whitgift Avenue house, so we sold the property reluctantly and he moved in with us.

The arrangement worked. Andrew liked having his 'Grandpa' to play games with and, typically, Dad kept himself to himself. The accommodation, though, was cramped, the steep staircase a problem and my unsociable hours on the radio hardly helped. A move to a larger property became the only answer when we were refused permission to build an extension to Kew Street.

In the *Evening Argus* we had read of a small terrace of run-down Regency houses which had been acquired for re-development by a local bookmaker, Victor Chandler. At one point, it had been intended to pull them down to make way for an extension to a bus garage, but local conservationists – backed by Lord Snowdon – protested, and after a public inquiry, the four houses in Charles Street were 'saved for the nation' and one of them, No. 22, became our next home in the summer of 1975.

It was a truly splendid building on five floors with two bathrooms, bow-fronted windows, a roof terrace and a fascinating history going back almost 200 years. It also had a ghost, as we discovered within weeks of moving in. Sylvia had been largely responsible for choosing the middle-of-terrace house because she liked the feel of the place compared with similar properties on either side. 'It just felt right for us,' she remembers now, 'There was something about No. 22 that appealed to me the moment I walked through the front door.'

Sylvia was not so certain, however, when she reported experiencing a very cold feeling in one part of the house – a sudden 'icy' moment in an otherwise centrally-heated building. Without checking, I dismissed the incident, putting it down either to an over-romantic imagination or, more likely, to a vicious draught caused by an open window. I didn't even bother to find out where the experience had happened – that is until days later when I was standing – for a moment – at the foot of the stairs in the narrow hall, talking to my father who had moved into the ground floor area with his own bedroom and lounge.

As Sylvia discovered, it's not easy to describe the phenomenon to others, but as Dad and I spoke I simply noted a dramatic change in the temperature around me. It was a momentary thing but quite enough for me to question Sylvia later in the day: Where had she been standing, I asked – perhaps hesitantly. You can guess the answer. 'In the hall,' she said, 'Where the stairs lead down to the basement kitchen area. Why?'

On another even more remarkable occasion in Charles Street – a summer's night as I recall – we had both been awoken in our third floor bedroom by what sounded like the scurrying of tiny feet, perhaps in a wall-space behind our double bed. Rats, mice, whatever it was – we were disturbed and both of us restive at this early hour. Suddenly – alarmingly – there was an almighty crash as the Teasmade tray complete with mugs flew into the air and onto the floor some distance from the chest of drawers upon which it had been standing !

No rational explanation for either of these incidents has ever been offered, although a spiritualist friend of a broadcasting colleague did visit us one afternoon and spoke of experiencing the presence of a spirit in the building which was untroubled and not malign. Years later, during a broadcast in an allegedly haunted pub in the Laines area of Brighton, I mentioned the icy feelings in my house to a psychic researcher who immediately asked where I was living.

'Charles Street,' I told him.

'Oh, No. 22?' he asked. 'It's a recognised ghost house, you know'.

'Don't you mean guest house?' I stammered.

'No, he replied.

Well that confirmed it for me, but we continued living there happily until 1987, and there were no other unexplained happenings.

Mind you – and this is weird too – the presence referred to by our spiritualist visitor could have been a member of my very own family. You may recall, earlier in the book, my astonishment at discovering that my grandfather's father, Thomas Henty, had been born 130 years before in a street close to where I had recently moved in 1971. Until that point I had been totally unaware of a Brighton connection.

Imagine my reaction then to learn from a second cousin who just happened to be a Radio Brighton listener, that there were strong Brighton links on my grandmother's side too, and they involved properties on

Marine Parade and – wait for it – Charles Street. Unbelievable? Well, I thought so too until I was presented with the facts.

Bear with me for a moment . . . My grandmother's maiden name was Kate Walker. She was one of eight children born to Cecil John Walker, a professional photographer, and his wife Caroline. His father was Cecil Sober Taylor Walker, who I gather was a commercial traveller and claimed to have invented washable wallpaper. He provides the first contact with Brighton on this side of the family, having been born in the town in 1813 at Marine Parade.

Cecil Sober Taylor's father was Charles William Walker who was born around 1786 and was a schoolmaster at the time of his marriage in 1807 to Cordelia Tuppen in Brighton. When his son was born he was entered in the register as a librarian of the Royal Marine Library (between Manchester Street and Charles Street on Marine Parade). The family also lived in Charles Street and Richmond Place, where he died in 1823 at the early age of 37. The library which opened in 1798 was initially run by Messrs. Donaldson and Wilkes, later by a Mr Pollard and subsequently 'by Messrs. Tuppen and Walker'. According to the book *The History and Architecture of Brighton*, 'Libraries were very important institutions in the Brighthelmstone of the day and in fact constituted the nearest approach to a pump room that the town has ever had'.

Incidentally Charles William Walker had written his own book entitled *Brighton and its environs* in 1807, and there are copies apparently in both Brighton and Worthing libraries today. His wife Cordelia was left with four sons under the age of 13 and may very well have continued running the library, which became known as Tuppen's Library.

So it could be argued that we were meant to move to Charles Street. My father had some independence, with his own 'quarters' - joining us for meals in the kitchen basement area. Andrew, happy at a local school, enjoyed his own room at the top, and Sylvia, who was by now working for a leading firm of solicitors, appreciated the variety of shops in St. James's Street and close proximity to the seafront and the Palace Pier.

For me though, while I valued a five-minute walk to work through the grounds of the Royal Pavilion, No. 22 – with its five floors – represented a spacious home for my 'bits and pieces'. On moving to Brighton in the early seventies my magpie tendencies had got slightly out of control. Then there were genuine antique shops, two establishments dealing in postcards, a woman who sold only pianolas, a thriving Saturday morning market in Gardner Street and several auction houses. It didn't take long for this inveterate collector to realise he was living in a 'knocker boys' nirvana'. Mary Belton sold me an upright pianola when we were living in Kew Street, where the garage was cleared to make room for it. Passing pedestrians must have thought Russ Conway had moved in as I pedalled furiously through Scott Joplin, Sousa Marches and a knee-trembling 1812 overture.

It survived the move across town too, but nearly killed a weighty removals man who eased its lowering into the basement by kneeling twixt piano and concrete floor. Getting it in was one thing; getting it out 12 years later was another, and to the best of my knowledge Mary's pianola is still there today – sold as an integral part of the freehold property in 1987. The ghost probably enjoys playing it from time to time.

Sylvia liked the pianola but she was far from happy when I purchased a vast juke box from a splendid shop called Rin Tin Tin. It didn't help matters either when she arrived home from work to discover the mega-object blocking what was admittedly a very narrow hallway. In her absence the shop owner and I had removed our solid front door to inch the mighty monster into the house, but turning left into the front lounge without removing another door had proved impossible – and that was when Mrs Henty appeared on the scene.

To Sylvia's eternal credit she has always given the thumbs-up to my, shall we say, 'mad magpie moments', but this was a 'no-joke' juke box and after a few Buddy Holly bursts and a snatch of Little Richard, back it went whence it came. She didn't object to a What The Butler Saw or Mutoscope which I spied in a North Road shop one Saturday morning. And the two telephone kiosks (each weighing three-quarters of a ton) were fine as long as someone else looked after them – like the excellent British Engineerium in Hove.

Sylvia even approved when I started to develop a passionate interest in another woman – or at least the artistic work of another woman – and that appreciation has grown over the years to such an extent that I am now regarded as the world's leading authority on the life and times of Mabel Lucie Attwell. Sylvia, needless to say, is a fan too. To quote our website, we're 'Mad About Mabel'.

32

Funnily enough, the skilled artistry of childrens' illustrator, Mabel Lucie Attwell (1879 – 1964) did not figure in my wartime childhood at all. There were 'Chicks Own' and 'Tiny Tots' annuals for sure but no work by Mrs Earnshaw (her married name). Postcards carried seaside views, not chubby children, and we kept our bathroom neat, tidy and dry without the need for the artist's ubiquitous bathroom plaque.

How then did I become so intrinsically involved in the fantasy world of Boo-Boos, Diddums dolls and general nursery nonsense? Well (takes deep breath . . .) it started when a listener to one of my record request programmes on Radio Brighton chose to use an Attwell postcard to convey her birthday greetings to a loved one. I commented – as one did in those unscripted days – that it was a very nice card and I liked the style, sentiment and industry of Mabel Lucie Wotsit. That did it! More schmaltzy cards followed, and in my travels around Brighton I began to discover that – in one shape or form – her creative work was everywhere.

Sylvia, me and one of my Mabel Lucie Attwell books. (Argus photograph)

There was a mushroom teapot in Bond Street for which I paid £12; postcards just off Kensington Gardens; a delightful cardboard plaque which suggested 'All The Nice Things To Do Are Naughty!' (this from another art-deco emporium in Bond Street); nursery china by Shelley in a cul-de-sac leading into North Road. Very soon I realised I was in touch with an icon, and as a journalist I wanted to know more – much more.

There were three children from her marriage to fellow illustrator, Harold Earnshaw, and I soon established that her only daughter, Peggy, was living in a large country house – the Old Rectory – at Froxfield, just outside the town of Marlborough in Wiltshire. Not only that, but she shared the house with the artist's surviving son, Peter. Both of them, however, appeared to be reluctant to speak to a journalist. Peter in particular was singularly unforthcoming and maintained – almost monotonously – that his famous mother 'would not have wanted the publicity'. Peggy, on the other hand, did not go along with this assertion, and eventually she did invite me to join the two of them for lunch in Froxfield.

I described our meeting in the book that was subsequently published in 1999 by Richard Dennis, *The Collectable World of Mabel Lucie Attwell* and here's an edited part of it:

'On the 29th October 1976, I set out from Brighton on the three-hour journey to Froxfield. Peggy was clearly not in the best of health. Her brother, Peter, pottered about in the background – keeping one ear on our conversation as he helped to prepare an informal lunch which we shared around the kitchen table. It was a cold day and the tape-recorded interview (later to be heard on BBC's 'Woman's Hour') took place in front of an open fire which snapped and crackled disconcertingly. Peggy patiently answered my questions, which she must have been asked many times before, with a gentle air of resignation. Did she recognise herself in any of her mother's illustrations? She replied: 'I find that a very hard question to answer. I don't think so. I know that some of the books were dedicated to us.'

I asked whether Peggy's childhood had been a happy one. After all, she described her mother as 'always working'. Her answer was emphatic: 'It was a very, very happy childhood. My mother was very good to us and very protective I'm sure, and perhaps a bit spoiling, but we were free to run in the fields, and wild flowers were everywhere then. It was excellent, just right. This was a new outlook about children; I think her friends and her generation were paying much more attention to their children and, if you like, spoiling them much more than their parents did.'

Was this reflected in her mother's work? 'She semed to be very original . . . one of the first people to use children as symbols for grown-ups with titles for grown-ups and to express things that grown-ups were feeling through these children.'

In the late 1950s, towards the end of her mother's career, Peggy took over responsibility for producing Mabel Lucie Attwell postcards, annuals and other work. When I showed Peggy some of her own cards from my collection, she was dismissive and told me they weren't worth keeping, 'Oh, you don't want to collect those', she chided. I gained the impression that she had been somewhat reluctant to take on the task of maintaining her mother's extraordinary output, knowing that she was an almost impossible act to follow. Peggy's final annual for Dean & Son under the Lucie Attwell banner was published in 1974.

As I got ready to leave the Old Rectory, I asked Peggy whether her mother would have been pleased by the renewed interest and enthusiasm for her work.

'I'm very, very sorry that she's missed it,' she replied. 'She began to have a little of it before she died. A young man came down and interviewed her for *Vogue*. I think he meant to come and make fun of her, but in fact it turned out to be a very nice interview indeed. And I said, after this, 'Hello – you're having a real comeback, aren't you ?' and she enjoyed that. I only wish she could see more of this going on now.'

Just before I left, Peggy spoke to me off the record. She was unwell, and she was concerned that because of this there might be no-one to organise a celebration of her mother's forthcoming centenary. She asked if

An appearance on Anglia Television's 'Bygones' programme, when presenter Dick Joice interviewed me about my Mabel Lucie Attwell connection and collection.

anything could be done. I was happy to reassure her, and on the 4th December, 1979, the Mabel Lucie Attwell Centenary Exhibition opened at Brighton Museum. Peter Earnshaw and other members of the family were there but, sadly, Peggy was not. She had died on the 30th November, 1978.'

My interest has never gone away, and happily the book continues to sell world-wide. There have been lecture tours to America, and the fine art auctioneers Christies consult me from time to time. I still attend postcard and antique fairs searching for original material and, of course, Sylvia and I did open the Mabel Lucie Attwell shop and museum in Fowey, Cornwall, in 1994.

More about that later, but meantime – back at the BBC – there were murmurs of discontent to be heard emerging from the Henty household. Time to try television perhaps – if you can call BBC South in Southampton television . . .

33

I was tempted to cry 'Whatever Happened to John Henty?' as I stared, disbelievingly, at the TV monitor screen. It was in the autumn of 1977. Earlier in the year, my father had collapsed and died outside our house in Charles Street, Brighton. In a bid to break free from what I regarded as the severe limitations of being a largish fish in a little local radio pond, I'd agreed to go on yet another BBC six-month attachment – this time to regional television in Southampton.

And it was here that producer John Frost persuaded me to take what was effectively a screen test. Without the aid or comfort of a visual teleprompter I rehearsed a piece to camera extolling the virtues of – yes, you've guessed it, Mabel Lucie Attwell. This meant learning the five-minute script and then putting it across in a convincing manner. As far as I was concerned, I failed on both counts. In an effort to remember my lines I spoke slowly and rather deliberately and this came across as plodding and ponderous.

I also appeared ill-at-ease (which I was) and painfully self-conscious. Talking confidingly into a microphone was one thing. Establishing a one-to-one relationship with an all-seeing eye was entirely another. I simply didn't recognise what I consider to be the real John Henty and although John Frost was supportive and spoke well of my subject matter, I knew then – at that very early stage – television was not for me.

A natural broadcaster? Yes, all the way, but Brighton's answer to Michael Parkinson? No – not even with a few helpful tips from my mate Desmond Lynam. So what to do at BBC South apart from watching their Peter Pan presenter Bruce Parker eat his lunch in the staff canteen? (A very popular place, by the way, where a good number of production people seemed to spend most of their days.)

At first I was assigned to the station's flagship daily programme 'South Today', and, in my experience, this only seemed to come alive after lunch when the half-empty production office would suddenly fill up with loads of people – all carrying clip-boards and talking across each other. I particularly remember one programme in the days leading up to Christmas 1977. In an effort to get the bearded bloke from Brighton more involved (that's me, folks) I was set the task of gathering in a range of Christmas essentials from nearby shops and market places.

From what I recall, the plan was to do a comparative piece to demonstrate that prices for crackers, mistletoe, nuts and the like had shot-up in the south over the past 12 months. Now on radio this would have been accomplished by one reporter wielding a tape-recorder and spending at most half-an-hour inside or outside the nearest local supermarket. On television, it required a cameraman shooting endless footage of Christmas shoppers complaining about what they had been told by the reporter and a dogsbody like me, belting around numerous shops to buy up the goodies so that comparative prices could be illustrated on screen.

What really amazed me though was the stampede of studio staff the moment the half-hour programme closed. They descended on the displayed goods like a swarm of locusts, and items from artichokes to azaleas just vanished into the thin – or perhaps that should be 'cold Southampton night'– air. I was genuinely gobsmacked. Why, even the presenters joined in and were seen rushing away with the odd bottle or two

and sprigs of holly flying everywhere. Gobsmacked? Yes. Disenchanted – certainly. There and then I decided that for me and my modest radio persona, regional television was not an option. If I had my way it was a case of 'South Today' – Gone Tomorrow! I'm a radio presenter: get me out of here.

So they did, but not before I completed a couple of TV documentaries which I very much enjoyed researching and in one case, presenting – under the careful guidance of John Frost. The first was a gentle piece tracing the work of the first world war poet, Edward Thomas, who had lived in Hampshire. His life and love for his wife Helen fascinated me, and it was a privilege to be

Not a bad likeness? A Brighton artist's tribute to a bearded DJ in the 1970s.

working on location in the calm countryside around Southampton which was so much a part of Thomas's tragically brief life.

The other documentary was a more up-beat production which aimed to tell the story of the Gurkha regiment which was – at that time – stationed in Church Crookham, not far from Aldershot. Here I did appear in front of the cameras from time to time and also recorded the accompanying commentary separately. Both programmes, I gather, were well received and seen throughout southern England. 'Ayo Gurkhali!' was even repeated on national television, although I never saw it – which is just as well.

A collector's item nevertheless. John Henty's television career encapsulated in just one magnificent hour, but whatever you do – DON'T BLINK while watching it.

I shall always be grateful to John Frost for taking me under his considerable wing all those years ago. Even on my inevitable return to Brighton, he maintained a regular contact, and yes, there was more TV work when we turned the spotlight on musicians in the Sussex town, namely Dome organist Douglas Reeve and the leader of the Pavilion trio, Ken Lyons. But what now for your roving radio reporter? Well this poem penned at the time seems to sum up my decision to go freelance – at the age of 42 – in September 1978:

> *I'm climbing down off my shelf*
> *To discover myself*
> *To shake hands with the man who is me*
> *I'm going out on a limb*
> *To encourage the 'him'*
> *Who has never become BBC.*
>
> *For ten years in the south*
> *I've been known as a mouth*
> *The spokesman that everyone hears*
>
> *Now it's time to say 'No'*
> *To switch off and go . . .*
> *For a mouth read a pair of keen ears.*

Clearly, it was not an easy decision to arrive at and was made even more difficult by the well-meaning advice of programme colleagues around me. One letter of resignation at least was torn up at the last moment and no doubt dear Sylvia – with her own job to contend with – must have grown weary of my continual debating the issues involved. As always though, she remained totally supportive of what I was hoping to achieve and with some encouragement from the acting programme organiser at what was now BBC Radio Sussex I finally took the plunge and handed yet another letter of resignation into the manager – the man who'd employed me in the first place, Bob Gunnell.

Despite our occasional differences, some of them fairly heated, Bob had always valued me as a good local broadcaster and I think he was proud of the progress made by one of his initial recruits. He promised that work on the station would still be available to me as a freelance, and this included the presentation of an early morning programme which came to be known as the Early Bird Show.

This, plus my links with Radio 2, public address work and travel-writing suggested that the bid for creative freedom expressed in my poem might not be quite as hazardous as others were wont to warn. Only one way to find out John, and on 1st January, 1979 that's precisely what I did. I headed a newsletter, intended to announce my move to the waiting millions: 'HERE'S HENTY!' and adopted the title JOHN HENTY UNLIMITED.

Well, I was now.

34

I suppose, appropriately enough, the Early Bird Show on BBC Radio Sussex could be described as representing my swan song on local radio. The final performance, so to speak, was broadcast on the morning of 1st May, 1987. It had been waking people up (or sending 'em back to sleep) on and off for several years. Even I cannot remember exactly when it all started – or how it came to have such an obvious title.

It was only a one-hour show and it ran between 5.30 and 6.30 when the main programme of the morning 'Good Morning Sussex' (see what I mean about titles) went on air. Despite the horrendous early start I thoroughly enjoyed presenting the EBS, and this is probably one of the main reasons why it almost developed into a cult show. Even a fellow broadcaster – DJ Mike Read, who lived just outside our catchment area – claimed to be hooked on it.

We all know the early morning can be a depressing time for those unable to sleep, in pain perhaps or simply tired of

**John Henty
The Early Bird Show
5.30am each weekday
on BBC Radio Sussex**

being alone. The Early Bird Show was fun, friendly and totally undemanding. It was also daft at times, deft and always there – ever-present – even on the morning of the Grand Hotel bomb in October 1984. Much of the mirthful mix had to be dropped that dreadful day, but I like to think regular listeners were reassured by our continued presence.

The mascot of the programme was a speaking worm called Whirly who claimed to live north of the town in Preston Park. We even took the programme there one summer morning when dozens of loyal listeners converged upon our lone radio car and joined in with the early bird chorus which included: 'GET UP, GET UP, GET UP AND OUT OF BED – GET UP, GET UP, GET UP YOU SLEEPY HEAD – FOR WE'RE THE EARLY BIRDS, THE BRIGHT'N EARLY BIRDS – LISTENING TO JOHN HENTY'S SHOW!' All together now . . .

On another classic occasion, we organised a 'sausage sizzle' on the beach between the two Brighton piers, and I will never forget the news reporter Rod Pounsett, in full barbecue gear, cooking the bangers and begging a couple of pints of milk from a passing milk float on the sunny seafront – all before six o'clock in the morning with a crowd of over a hundred listeners, young and old alike. Hardly the Radio One Roadshow, but magical nonetheless.

Another popular feature, when phone-ins were becoming all the rage on radio, was the Early Bird phone-out. On my travels around Sussex, if I spotted a telephone kiosk in a particularly out-of-the-way location I would note down its number and then invite listeners in a subsequent programme to search for it – and be there when I rang from the studio. Amazingly, despite the early hour and often hideous weather conditions, this never failed to produce a result.

I even tried the same trick on a Sunday morning show, when instead of choosing a Sussex callbox I rang a kiosk which I had noted on a holiday in the Scottish Highlands weeks before. At first there was no reply from the delightfully-named Plockton community, but then – just as I was about to write the item off – a puzzled Scottish voice was heard to plaintively answer . . . 'Hello!'. It was a passing cyclist. He'd heard the phone ringing, picked it up and found himself talking to thousands of people a good six hundred miles away on the south coast of England. Good radio – even if British Telecom were not wildly amused by the 'mis-use' of their kiosks,

Regular listeners to the Early Bird Show needed no prompting to ring the studio in the early hours. They knew, of course, that I was the only person in the vast building for at least the first 20 minutes of the show. I would refer to the miniature keyboard on my desk lighting up as the phones rang and occasionally – at random and between records – I would answer the odd call or two.

One such caller was an older man who identified himself simply as Eric. He was in his seventies, still travelled to work as some form of courier for a travel agency in London and was not in the best of health. However, he was always more concerned about *my* well-being, and I only needed to sound ever-so-slightly down or weary for Eric to be on the blower with an anxious

'Are you OK John? You sound rather depressed this morning.'

'I'm fine Eric – just a bit damp from the rain, but thanks for your call. And now here's Herb Alpert and his Tijuana Brass.'

This happened on a regular basis until one day when the dear fellow, whom I'd never met, casually mentioned that he would be away for a spell undergoing a serious operation. I sensed that Eric was suffering from a form of cancer, but in the few seconds available to me I was only able to reassure him briefly and insist that he returned to Brighton as soon as possible.

'I can't afford to lose any listeners' I joked, 'You get well again Eric – the Early Birds need you, and so do I.'

Well, happily he did just that, and soon I was getting the cheering messages again in the middle of Queen Ida's Zydeco music (popular with listeners) and bursts of the Early Bird chorus, sung by the man who wrote it – my good friend, Miles Wootton. We had a quote for the day, a musical star of the week, we adopted a duck at some wild life centre in Gloucestershire (named 'Mrs Feather' in a daft competition) and occasionally I would get a long-range weather forecast exclusively for the show by ringing a man called Bill in Yorkshire who used frog spawn amongst other things to make his unusual predictions.

Does it sound like fun? Well, let me tell you, it *was* fun. By and large, I was left to my own devices. The pay was pathetic but with the early start, it did allow me to get on with other more lucrative freelance activities during the day. I recorded middle of the night pieces for Radio 2 on a weekly basis. I represented the BBC on its stand at the Daily Mail Ideal Home Exhibition for two years and I continued to provide the public address at Selhurst Park for Crystal Palace and Wimbledon, with the occasional stint at the Goldstone Ground for Brighton and Hove Albion.

At the radio station though, things were beginning to wobble, and it wasn't just the new receptionist's bosom – 'Good morning. I've come to be inter . . . good gracious!' No, worse. A new manager had been appointed to replace the innovative Bob Gunnell who was retiring. I have to say that Bob, not surprisingly, proceeded to re-write the rules for this enforced removal and threw himself into community-related activities with commendable gusto.

Meantime, the new broom, whom I would prefer not to name, set about sweeping clean the corridors of Marlborough Place, and I knew it was only a matter of time before he would be knocking on the door of my office. (Well, cupboard – er, corner of the gramophone library, actually.) The programme organiser, Nigel Kay, who was destined for bigger and better things in the years ahead, was a forceful yet friendly character who – happily – liked the Early Bird format and initially became its champion.

Not for long, though. Mr Broomhead had his own ideas and decided – in the spring of 1987 – to (as the Evening Argus so delicately put it) 'AXE JOHN HENTY' and the Early Bird Show as well. I lived five minutes away from the radio station. Our clean-sweeping friend chose to ring me at home with the news and really offered no convincing explanation for his decision apart from some mumbled reference to 'budgetary considerations'.

I was not surprised, but then I was not amused – and neither, of course, were my faithful listeners. Eric in particular was incensed and immediately set about raising a petition, writing to all local MPs and ringing the manager.

Did he succeed in his one-man campaign against a BBC decision ? Well, what do you think ?

35

Ifind it deeply ironical really that on the morning of my final Early Bird Show on BBC Radio Sussex – Friday, 1st May, 1987 – a letter was being prepared at No. 10 Downing Street in reply to a certain Mr E.G Muggeridge of Brighton. Yes, Eric had decided, in his frustration, to address the prime minister, Margaret Thatcher, personally. What was she going to do about the situation in Brighton? And he didn't mean refurbishment of the Grand Hotel or reinstatement of the wobbly West Pier. Mr Muggeridge of Brighton was referring to the dubious demise of a certain John Henty!

The reply from number ten read: 'Mrs Thatcher hopes you will understand that, as the matter you raise is the responsibility of one of the principal government departments, she has asked that your letter is forwarded to that department so that they may reply to you direct on her behalf.'

Fifteen days later, with the programme now off air, a Miss Macfarlane wrote to suggest 'It is a matter for the BBC alone to decide what programmes should be broadcast on its channels and to decide what time of the day or evening particular programmes should be shown [sic].' So that's all right, then.

At this point, no doubt, Eric probably shrugged his shoulders and gave up the fight, as I had done – albeit weeks earlier. He'd have enjoyed the final 60 minutes though, because I used the time to go through all the usual nonsense with Whirly, Bill's weather forecast, an Early Bird chorus or two and some very carefully chosen music. There was 'W.O.L.D' by Harry Chapin, 'Shine Silently' by Nils Lofgren, 'I Only Want To Be With You' by Southside Johnny and The Asbury Jukes. Bucks Fizz sang 'Now Those Days Are Gone' unaccompanied and Little Richard ended the show with 'Somebody Cares'.

Jean in Rottingdean cared. She wrote two days later: 'Tears came into my eyes when you played 'Somebody Cares' and said a quiet 'Goodbye' last Friday. I have enjoyed your cheerful chatter so very much and waking up will not be the same now.' It wasn't the same for Eric, either. Remember, we had never met, but 10 months later I noted in the *Evening Argus* a news item which reported the death on 2nd March, 1988, of the brother of TV personality Malcolm Muggeridge. Eric George Muggeridge was described as the founder of Foster Parents Plan in 1937 and in the book of remembrance at Brighton's Downs Crematorium are these words: 'Almost eighty-two years he brightened this earth with his deep love and kindness, great humour and mirth. His courage saved thousands of children in need; Ever humble and earnest – yet a great man indeed.'

I will always remember Eric as my listener and, happily, I am still in touch with his charming daughter, Maureen, who lives today in Western Australia. But what of the redundant radio raconteur? you ask. A milk-round perhaps would make sense at that early hour or maybe an all-night shift in the main Brighton post office. Sylvia and I had our own ideas, and the first was to move away from the centre of Brighton and eastwards to the county town of East Sussex, Lewes.

Charles Street, close by the Palace Pier, had become a little too raunchy for our taste and, while we enjoyed the close proximity to the seafront, we

A slice of 'Bread' for Nice 'n' Easy – an opportunity to interview (L to R) Graham Bickley, Melanie Hill and Jean Boht from the hit television comedy during a summer season in Bournemouth.

didn't appreciate the two pubs at the end of the street and boozy parties on our own doorstep nightly. In addition I was keen to find a property where I could construct my own radio studio and start producing half-hour versions of the Early Bird Show for a hospital radio audience right across the United Kingdom.

Backed by British Telecom, 'Nice 'n' Easy' was available then on an audio cassette which contained two programmes – one on each side of the tape. The thinking behind the project was based on my early experiences in hospital radio in Croydon. Record requests and bingo sessions were the main part of the station's output – with the occasional outside broadcast and celebrity interviews thrown in – but anything more ambitious was out of the question for financial reasons.

'Nice 'n' Easy' provided that additional programming and, thanks to BT, was available to any hospital radio group free of charge. It ran for over five years (352 editions) and in that time carried interviews with a wide range of top celebrities including Charlton Heston (remember?), Petula Clark, Cilla Black, Catherine Cookson, Ken Dodd, Jimmy Greaves, Denis Healey and an 'exclusive' with Cliff Richard.

It also had a weekly quiz, travel with ITV's John Carter, gardening with Bert and lots of ecletic music. All this from a garage space adjoining the modest property we acquired in laid-back Lewes in the autumn of 1987. And when I say 'modest' I mean that it was tiny compared with the five floors we had available to us in Charles Street. Bad news for the magpie tendency and, of course, for the growing collection of slot machines, children's annuals and Mabel Lucie Attwell miscellanea.

Initially, a large loft came to the rescue, but as far as I was concerned this was only a short-term answer. It was essential to find a more permanent home where the items could be displayed and enjoyed by other people – for I had growing evidence of a revived interest in the work of Ms Attwell, especially in America, and this prompted the thought of a book.

The London gallery-owner Chris Beetles had produced a profusely illustrated tribute to the artist in 1988 but, inevitably, it concentrated on her book illustrations and to a large extent ignored her amazing output of work on behalf of postcard manufacturers, Valentines of Dundee. Being a postcard collector myself, I realised that there was now a need for a more comprehensive publication which would go into greater detail about her 'lively life' and provide a full breakdown of her postcard output from before the first world war through to the middle 1950s.

Happily, west country publisher Richard Dennis agreed with me, and I was commissioned to write what became known as *The Collectable World of Mabel Lucie Attwell* in 1994. I was able to use my earlier interviews with her children, Peggy Wickham and Peter Earnshaw. On Peggy's death I also came to know her two sons John and Mark Wickham, and through them I discovered that their grandmother had spent the last 20 years of her life in the attractive town of Fowey, on the south coast of Cornwall.

Although I had enjoyed a touring holiday to Cornwall in the early 1960s, it was largely unfamiliar territory to me and so I was certainly venturing into the unknown when I stepped off the Great Western train from Paddington to Par station on the afternoon of Monday, 4th July, 1994. The plan was to visit the house – high above the town – where Mrs Earnshaw lived with her son, Peter, just after the war. She carried on with her illustrative work from a room at the rear of No. 3 St. Fimbarrus Road while Peter acted as her secretary and ran errands to Fore Street and bought provisions at Varcos on the corner of the Esplanade.

While she rarely ventured into the centre of the small town, Peter spent much of his time down there and was welcomed in most of the pubs for his generosity, piano playing and sociable nature. He was nicknamed 'the Colonel' and made frequent excursions across the harbour to Polruan.

On my first visit, a single-decker bus from St Austell eventually turned up at Par station, and within 15 minutes I was walking down into the town from the Safe Harbour bus-stop. My first impressions were most favourable, and I thought to myself – no wonder the shrewd Mabel Lucie Attwell decided to move here from London in 1945. I wrote in my diary: 'Visually – a joy. Steep, winding paths. A ferry across to Polruan – small pubs, restaurants etc.' In other words, the place had 'appeal', and I was not surprised to learn that over the years other notable literary figures had also chosen to live in and around Fowey. Daphne Du Maurier, for example, was certainly known to Mrs Earnshaw, and they renewed their casual friendship in the town immediately after the war.

During my short stay I met Beryl Delve, a community nurse from Liverpool, who cared for Mabel Lucie Attwell in the final months of the artist's life. Francis Carne, a delightful character, who had lived his entire life in Fowey, told me how he provided curtains and fittings for the couple at No. 3 St. Fimbarrus. A woman living in a house overlooking the harbour showed me Christmas cards she had been sent by the artist and one older man from Polruan remembered painting and decorating her house on more than one occasion.

My research for the book was going very well indeed, and I promised myself a day off to go on a circular walk from the Bodinnick car ferry at one end of town to the Polruan passenger ferry at the other. The 'Hall Walk', as it is known, has been described as one of the most beautiful walks in the entire country and I would not argue with that description. At the end of it I decided on a Cornish cream tea and headed for a small tea room which I'd noted on my frequent forays through Fore Street. Here, amid warm scones and against a background of incongruous oom-pah music, I discussed my plans with the owner – a jolly German woman – who clearly warmed to me in the same way that I appreciated her home-made apfelstrudel.

When I mentioned my collection of Mabel memorabilia and the need to find a permanent home for it, she enthusiastically pointed out that the property next door – a former fashion shop – was on the market and would make a good location for a museum and shop. She also added that there was sizeable accommodation above so we could even live over the shop, so to speak. What Marie did not say, however, was that No. 34 Fore Street had been on the market for more than a year and would require a fair amount of refurbishment and re-structuring to make it viable as a shop and liveable in as a second home.

And how would Sylvia – back in Lewes – react to this sudden, seemingly dramatic change in her ordered life-style? There was only one way to find out. I collected the agent's details for the freehold building, completed my research notes and headed for home.

On the first of April, 1996 (yes, I know), the Mabel Lucie Attwell Museum and Shop opened at No. 34 Fore Street in Fowey. It had the title: 'Please Remember – Don't Forget'. On 23rd March, 1999, Richard Dennis Publications launched *The Collectable World of Mabel Lucie Attwell* at the Chris Beetles Gallery in London. The book was written in Fowey.

36

'Make sure your enthusiasm is shared by others and that there are thousands of 'em!' That was the one piece of advice I gave to anyone who'd been round our modest museum and commented that 'it must be great' to be able to put your collection of whatever on display to the general public. We had Rupert Bear nuts, Beano and Dandy fanatics, motor-bike enthusiasts and hoarders of anything Hornby – you name it, they all found their way, eventually, to No. 34 Fore Street, Fowey.

And, with very few exceptions, they liked what they saw. We'd gone to a lot of trouble and expense to create a lively tribute to the artistry of Mabel Lucie Attwell. There were hundreds of her postcards, cabinets full of china, books and biscuit tins, family photographs and examples of her work achieved while living in the town.

Probably the most popular item on display was a humble bathroom plaque in pristine condition which brought back memories for numerous visitors, many of whom could faultlessly recite the warning message, word for word: 'Please remember – Don't forget – Never leave the bathroom <u>wet</u> – Nor leave the soap still in the water – That's a thing we <u>never</u> ought'er.'

I spent countless hours listening to stories associated with the oh-so-pertinent plaque – boarding school bathrooms, Blackpool B&Bs, fastidious grannies and even examples of the message being received and understood in faraway outposts of the British Empire.

One morning – well before opening time – there was a loud banging on our front door. Remember, we lived above the shop. I threw open our kitchen window on the first floor and noted a young, well-dressed woman who immediately shouted to me in an almost hysterical voice, 'I must have one of those bathroom plaques in the window. I'm flying back to South Africa later today and we're just about to leave for Heathrow Airport – can you help?'

Well, I could and I did. We opened the museum shop specially for her and from what I remember she purchased more than one copy and also some other Mabel mementoes. She was a satisfied customer, but others were not so easily pleased. In our first year one woman wanted to know what the exhibition was all about. I patiently explained that it was a permanent tribute to a quite remarkable woman who had lived in Fowey for the last 20 years of her life and was famous all over the world for her artwork.

Not in Bletchley, it seemed. The woman was unmoved.

'It's in there, is it?' she asked.

'Yes,' I said, 'A full scale display of all Mabel Lucie's creativity – very colourful and lots of fun. There's a small charge to go round.'

Sharp intake of breath from Mrs. Bletchley: 'Ooooh, I'm not paying to go round,' she trumpetted, 'Not after what we've just paid in the car park!'

Somewhat exasperated by this last remark, I found myself replying, 'Well, I'll tell you what dear' (careful John – remember you're the curator of this mini museum) 'You come on a bicycle next time and you'll be able to afford our exhibition, won't you?'

Exit one indignant lady from Buckinghamshire.

Sadly she was not untypical, especially during the peak summer months, and in time, Sylvia and I decided to offer free admission to the museum in the hope that sales in the shop would compensate for the short-fall in museum income. I enjoyed the day to day responsibility of running the shop, though. For me it was a novelty and there was an element of show business about it. – the repartee, the sales patter, the novelty conjuring tricks and meeting people from all over the world.

We had our fair share of celebrities, too. Gloria Hunniford and her daughter, Caron Keating, were regular visitors to Fowey and would often pop in. Esther Rantzen arrived one crowded afternoon with husband Desmond Wilcox in tow. Then there was the ginger-haired BBC correspondent, Nicholas Witchell, with his wife and children, and that actor fellow who's always on the box – you know . . . Warren Clarke. Oh, they all liked the small town friendliness of Fowey and its relaxed informality. They got a warm welcome in our shop too – even if Sylvia didn't immediately recognise them.

For her, running a shop was far from being a novelty. Sylvia's parents had always been in business for themselves and she recalled helping in her father's sub-post office in Beckenham and the all-pervasive smell of frying when he opened a popular fish and chip emporium on the outskirts of Croydon.

The other problem with running a shop seven days a week for a good six months of the year was that we very rarely had any time to do anything else or go anywhere else. Friends in Sussex would frequently say how nice it must be to spend so much time in Cornwall. We would quickly point out that we saw very little of our westernmost county and could just as easily have been running a business in Croydon or Carlisle. One main street shopping centre was very much like another, we argued – although, to be fair, Fore Street, Fowey, certainly had some ancient buildings and the attractions of the bustling town quay at one end. We got on well with our fellow traders and I think they appreciated us because they recognised that Mabel Lucie Attwell had been an important figure in the world of childrens' fiction and her late association with the town was worthy of celebration. The museum was just that, and everybody was impressed by its professional approach and attractive layout.

It did have a 'shelf-life', though. Undoubtedly, the most successful museums are those which regularly change, update and freshen their exhibits. With ours, this proved difficult. One year we accommodated a woman's Rupert the Bear collection which did create some interest, but apart from the occasional new Attwell acquisition, our basic presentation remained much the same and, consequently, numbers going round the museum began to drop.

We reckoned that people return to Cornwall on a regular basis for their annual holidays and the majority adopt a 'Been there, done that, bought the T-shirt' approach. In other words, familiarity can breed contempt as well as content. Perhaps it was time to move on or just concentrate on the shop, which was by now – 1999 – doing well enough in its own right. And, happily, we had a new item to sell – signed, hard-back copies of the Richard Dennis book.

Sylvia, in particular, felt that we should close the museum – pointing out that the book would effectively take its place. After all, hadn't we done enough to promote the life and times of someone else's grandmother? I found myself agreeing with her, and in due time, we closed both the shop and the museum but retained the living accommodation above. A pet shop run by a local man replaced our business venture, and we took a cabinet in a nearby antiques emporium to sell our Mabel items and Hornby train pieces.

Trips to Fowey from Lewes became a regular part of our new routine and we even took a party of Attwell fanatics down to stay at the lovely Fowey Hotel for a weekend of Mabel Musing in February 2003. Meantime, I had developed a new interest, or re-discovered an old one – British music hall and the sheer artistry of Brighton's own Cheeky Chappie – the one and only Max Miller.

Sylvia's heart must have sunk when she learned that, not content with extolling the virtuosity of a deceased children's illustrator, I was now about to promote the unrivalled professionalism of a British stand-up comedian who had died in 1963. Yes, I had accepted the role of chairman of the Max Miller Appreciation Society under its president, the Croydon-born Roy Hudd OBE – almost full-circle you might say, and as good a time as any to bring this elongated, episodic journal to a temporary close.

I say 'temporary' because I feel obliged here to adopt the term used by journalists when reporting on the second day of a lengthy trial: 'The case continues . . .' So it does, and I've not even mentioned appearing on 'Double Your Money' with a chimpanzee, circus pony and Hughie Green; Spending the night with the light house keeper on the island of Sark and visiting a lap-dancing club with John Craven of 'Newsround' in Newfoundland. Never mind.

There's more to come of this I'm sure but at least now, when the little ol' lady on a No. 2 bus to Shoreham asks the driver 'Whatever happened to that John Henty?' he'll be able to say: 'Don't ask me, love – I'm not normally on this route . . . but I *have* read the book.'

And so have you. Thank you!

Roy Hudd OBE is president of the Max Miller Appreciation Society and a fellow Croydonian. Here I'm congratulating him the day after he received his well-deserved gong.

Epilogue

If there's a life-sized bronze statue to Max Miller in Brighton; if the crowd at a Crystal Palace home game still sings 'Glad All Over'; if you ever see a bathroom plaque beseeching you to 'Never Leave The Bathroom <u>Wet</u>'; and, finally, if there's a bloody great pianola in the basement of a house in Charles Street, Brighton, which plays the 1812 Overture all by itself – then, having read this book, you'll know why.

Desert Island Discs

For the benefit of BBC researchers everywhere, and especially those working on Radio 4's 'Desert Island Discs' programme, these are the eight gramophone records I would take with me for my castaway life – with Sue Lawley, of course.

Peanut Vendor; Stan Kenton Orchestra (My first taste of big band music)
Glad All Over; Dave Clark Five (Crystal Palace 'theme')
My Guy; Mary Wells (Sylvia and me, 1964)
Unchained Melody; The Goons (The Goons and Peter Sellers)
Shine Silently; Nils Lofgren (Beautiful: says it all)
I've Been Working Too Hard; Southside Johnny and the Jukes
                              (Great rock 'n roll out of Chicago)
W.O.L.D; Harry Chapin (Early morning radio)
Think About Me; The Tubes (West Coast California 1970s)

My one book: *The Hentys – an Australian Colonial Tapestry,* by Marnie Bassett. A clear indication that Hentys know how to survive under difficult circumstances.

My one luxury: A coin-operated Allwin slot machine with lots of pennies.

Worth craning your neck for – a favourite cartoon of mine, reproduced with the kind permission of the artist, Patrick Wright.

Henty's Crossword Puzzle

ACROSS

1 John stayed here with the Yarwood family on America's West Coast (8)

5 The Early Bird Show started around this time most mornings (4)

8 Put your hands together, folks, for this (8)

9 McCartney shares this with Foot and Getty (4)

11 Time off during National Service (5)

12 John heard from this 28-year-old, concerned about his 'boys' (7)

13 No condition to be in when appearing on BBC South TV (6)

15 John collects the telephone variety (6)

18 Saint for the unsighted (7)

19 A big one on most streets in Brighton (5)

21 The middle of this for Radio Brighton's music policy (4)

22 John's public school prompted private thoughts (8)

23 John's incongruous Uncle Harry on the West Coast (4)

24 News passed on this way: primated (*anagram*) (8)

DOWN

1 En route for Stockholm in October 1963 – thanks to John (7)
2 Mrs Hook in New Addington was this society's auxiliary secretary (5)
3 To make things even worse (10)
4 Happened afterwards (6)
6 The Early Show does this to its audience – hopefully (7)
7 Sisters in harmony from this Irish family – John met Linda! (5)
10 Gracie had the biggest one in the world! (10)
14 As a child, John read these year by year (7)
16 This sort of labour worked very long hours –not for the BBC, though (7)
17 'Glad All Over' became one of these at Selhurst Park, London (6)
18 A lament for the dead (5)
20 For a short time John was in this state in Santa Barbara (*colloquial*) (5)

[*Solution below*]

Name-dropping Index

I've had my photograph taken
I've 'ad me photo took,
I've muttered 'cheese'
I've clenched me knees –
Now you can 'ave a look!

John, Shell Photographic Unit, 1958

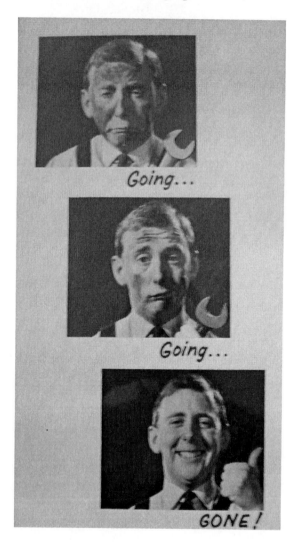